MW00715208

I

When Big Boys Tri

It's not the race – it's the journey

Michael Pate

Copyright © 2003 by Michael Pate
First Edition

All rights reserved. No part of this book shall be
reproduced, stored in retrieval systems, or transmitted
by any means without written permission from Michael
Pate.

ISBN: 1-59196-256-0

This book is not intended to be a substitute for medical
advice. If there are any doubts in your mind about the
advisability of undertaking training for a triathlon or
any other workout activity, you should consult a
physician.

Table of Contents

Acknowledgements...

First of all I owe everything that I have to God. Without Him, I would be nothing. With Him, I am everything. I couldn't get up and go to work and face the world if I had to face it without Him.

Many thanks go to my wife who doesn't mind the alarm going off at 5:00 a.m. on a school day and giving me that little nudge to get out of bed in the morning to get to the pool. You have helped me find myself and you have supported me in every decision I have made. Even with the wrong ones, you have stood by my side. No man could ask to have a wife as great as you. I love you and always will.

My inspiration comes in the form of a little blonde-headed boy named Christopher. To hear him screaming, "Daddy, I love you!" in the transition of a triathlon gives it all new meaning. Thanks for loving Daddy just the way he is.

To my late Father, thanks for instilling in me the values of God, Church, and Family. I never heard you say that you couldn't do anything, and if you didn't know how, you managed to figure it out. I just wish you could have been there when I crossed the finish line the first time.

To my Mother, you are incredible. You are always able to find the good in everyone you meet and you think I am perfect.

To my in-laws, thanks for being my second family.

Brad, Jay, and Jeff, I don't know how you guys ever got me hooked on this sport, but thanks.

Red River Tri Club, you are an awesome group of people that I am happy to be associated with.

Mike at Red River Cyclery, thanks for taking care of me and my bike.

Jay, Kimberly, Robin, Stacy, Steve, and Payne, thanks for being my "Test Market".

Mark Davis, Xbigman.com - "YOU DA MAN"

Special thanks to Mr. Arnold Palmer for personally granting permission to use his poem.

Preface

I honestly didn't start out to write a book. I started out keeping a journal for my own benefit, to remind myself where I started. Yeah, maybe it was a crazy notion to have the goal of finishing a triathlon, but two years later, I am still working out, losing weight and entering triathlons. I am not a super-stud athlete by any stretch of the imagination, but I am a finisher. Triathlons are not just for elite athletes; they are for people of all sizes, shapes, colors and genders.

I am just a big guy who made a decision to change his life, one step at a time. My whole purpose of sharing my story with you is to show you that it can be done. If my story inspires you to make that same life change, then it has been worth it all to expose my personal feelings and thoughts with you. I am nowhere near the end of my journey and I am probably only starting in the eyes of some, but every day brings me little closer to reaching my goals.

There is no better time to start than today.

THE MAN WHO THINKS HE CAN

If you think you are beaten, you are.
If you think that you dare not, you don't.
If you'd like to win, but you think you can't,
It's almost certain you won't.

If you think you'll lose, you've lost,
For out in the world you'll find
Success begins with a fellow's will.
It's all in the state of mind.

If you think you are outclassed, you are.
You've got to think high to rise.
You've got to be sure of yourself before
You can ever win a prize.
Life's battles don't always go
To the stronger or faster man,
But soon or later the man who wins
Is the man who thinks he can."

–Arnold Palmer –

- Chapter One -
The Tri That Made Me Try

It was a cool morning in June of 2001, and the sound company of which I am part-owner had been hired to provide sound and music for a triathlon. The Central Louisiana venue was Indian Creek. Indian Creek is a beautiful setting in June, partly due to the fact that this is one of Louisiana's more mature recreational areas. The large trees and natural landscape make a gorgeous setting for any event, whether it is a family reunion or sporting event.

I had never been to a triathlon and didn't really know what to expect. Because of my friendship with the race director and several of the organizers, we had just happened onto this gig. Since we had no experience providing sound for a triathlon we made the decision to go out the day before and set up so we wouldn't be rushed the morning of the triathlon.

That morning came and I was sweating my 368-pound butt off getting things lined up for what I thought would happen. In my own way, I hoped to be invisible to the elite athletes that were sure to be at this event with their flat stomachs and low body fat counts.

The first thirty minutes were a blur to me as I chased after the race director to capture his wireless microphone and hand it off to the announcer. I was exhausted running around the transition area. To paint a picture for you of what this was like, I felt like I had an imaginary bungee cord that connected me to the race director. He would go running off and would get about twenty-five yards away and there I would go chasing him again. As I built up speed and got near him, he would take off in another direction and off I would go again. Since this was the inaugural event, the race director was trying to make sure everything was taken care of and was very popular among the volunteers who were full of questions.

I can still remember how the excitement started to build among the triathletes as time drew near for the first wave to begin. Each would check and recheck the layout of his transition area. If you have never been to a triathlon before, let me explain what a transition area is. Most of these events have areas that are laid out with racks for each competitor's bike. Each competitor will lay out this area in his own special way so that it will speed up his transition. Some may have a towel spread out on the ground so that they will have a clean place to step. Most of the racers will have a extra bottle of water so they can wash the dirt off their feet before putting on their bike shoes. Some will have a small, water-filled Rubbermaid container just large enough for their feet to fit in. Also on the towel, they will have their running shoes with their race bib number underneath so the wind won't blow the bib away. If they choose to wear a shirt during the bike portion, they will have their shirt draped over their bike and their helmet placed on their handlebars. Each of these competitors was so meticulous about this. Later I would understand that this was so they would be able to make a quick and efficient transition through each event.

A pre-race meeting was to be held for first-time triathletes, which was a nice touch. This was great to help calm the nerves of those first-time participants and it also would let each one know that there were some other "first-timers" here. As the newbies gathered together, you could see them obviously sizing up the competition. Little did they know that the real competition was between their ears and not standing next to them. This particular event had a professional triathlete there to walk the first-timers through what they should expect. Now at the time, this was just interesting to me, and I listened and took it in. Among my friends, I am famous for the excess amount of useless information that I store in my brain. I know about things that I really have no reason to know and most of it is trivial, but I tend to pick up on the little things - much like the things being told to these athletes. I remembered that the pro tried to calm their fears about unknown things being in the water with the justification that the first swimmers in the water would scare anything off to the other side of the lake when they came splashing through. He also told them that if this was their first triathlon that they should just face the fact that they weren't going to place first. He explained that when the gun sounded for the start, they should just hang back for about fifteen seconds and let everybody else go and then just fall in. He warned them that if they jumped up in the middle of the start that it could get a little rough. As far as the biking portion of the race, they were informed that they would need to ride smart and keep their eyes on the road and other bikers. It was a lot of useful information that should have relieved some of their anxiety.

As the start time grew near, triathletes entered the lake to acclimate themselves to the water temperature and to start warming up. Some of them were actually swimming halfway out on the course to warm up. I was just thinking that they were wasting a lot of unnecessary energy and they should save some for what they had to do later. Some people had on their game faces and others had on faces of fear and doubt. I have to admit I was scared for some of the swimmers as I looked out over the swim course. It looked like an extremely long distance. The swim usually starts in segments called "waves" if there are a fairly large number of competitors. What this amounts to is a staggered start that usually puts the elite or seeded athletes starting the race first, then a few minutes later, the next wave will start with whatever division the race director has deemed. The race starts and the first wave is off and gone, then the second wave, then the third and finally the fourth wave.

As one of the waves started, several of us formed into a group on the shore to watch a swim start in a triathlon for the first time. Things seemed to be going fine but then about one hundred yards off the shore, I saw a swimmer making his way to the nearest rescue boat. One of the gentlemen on the shore had a pair of binoculars and told me who it was. It ended up that he had gotten in the middle of the wave and was kicked in the head and had become disoriented and panicked in the water. Now I don't tell this story to embarrass the guy who got into the rescue boat because he is a friend of mine, but even though I didn't know it then, it would play an important part in my life later. This guy is in great shape so this event showed me that the swim is, for most people, the toughest event in a triathlon and should be taken seriously.

As swimmers began to exit the water and I looked out over the buoys in the lake, I couldn't imagine why on earth anyone would want to swim out in the middle of the lake and come back. I didn't think I could swim out to the start of the race much less that distance. I even remember telling a member of the rescue team "if I came up missing, you could just look about 20 yards off the beach and that's probably where I went down." The first racers out of the water were just what I had expected: those little bitty guys with zero-percent body fat. But as time passed, I realized that people were getting out of the water who weren't the zero-percent body fat folks. They were your average, everyday Joe. What I didn't understand is that each one had a big smile on his face, as if to say, "I did it!"

As more racers came out of the water, I moved over to the bike transition area. Some of the competitors would exit the swim and sprint to the transition area and some would just take their time and do a little deep breathing exercise, which in my opinion was totally warranted. For the most part, each person seemed to have an art to his or her movement. Each move was intentional, and almost preplanned. How and why were they so deliberate? I was thinking, "Just put your helmet on and get on your bike and go!" These folks were putting on shoes and permanently attaching themselves to the bike. Now I was sure that they were crazy. But one by one, they left the bike transition area and soon it was empty. In a triathlon, there is usually an area that will be designated as a mount and dismount area. Each competitor must pass into this area before he can get on his bicycle and must stop and dismount his bike before he exits this area coming back in off the bike course.

As the faster bikers started to arrive from their little twenty-mile stint, I had starting building a rapport with the announcer. I shared with him that these people just had to be crazy. Just doing *one* of the three events alone should get you a free membership in the crazy club. When the first competitor came in off the bike ride, he was going so fast that he locked up his rear brake about thirty feet from the dismount area and his rear tire was smoking by the time he stopped. This guy was flying on his bike. Then into the dismount area comes this guy who is pretty bowed up, and the announcer tells me, "You see that guy? He use to be a really big guy and now he is one of the better triathletes in the state." Okay, this got my attention. This guy used to be a big guy and now he looks like he does. That just didn't happen overnight with the latest diet from Hollywood. The announcer said, no, it didn't happen overnight, but it happened. At that moment, somewhere in my subconscious, I had to be thinking, "I could do it if he did it." But I was still sure that these people were crazy. I watched a few more of the bikers come in and then we moved over to the finish line, where the last leg of the event, the run, would end.

It was when I was standing at the finish line that I started to come to the realization that ninety-percent of these people weren't crazy. Most of them were not competing against the clock, not against someone else - they were competing against themselves. It didn't matter if they didn't place in their age group. They had finished and in their minds, they were winners. More and more people that I thought I could relate to started crossing the finish line and then, from around the corner came a bigger guy, not as big as me and he may have never been as big as me, but big guy. He was giving it all he had and headed toward the finish line. At that moment, the announcer said "And here comes our first Clydesdale!" Now keep in mind that I knew nothing about this race except they would award age group awards, I didn't know that some races had Clydesdale Divisions. The Clydesdale, or in some events, the Rhino division is usually for guys who weigh two-hundred and one pounds and over. The ladies' class is called the Athena division and is for female competitors who are 150 pounds and over. By the way, this race didn't have a Clyde Division, so I just thought "Clydesdale" was some big insult. I turned to the announcer and thought, "Look you idiot, this guy may be a big guy, but he's doing more than your lazy butt. Why would anybody want to come out and run a race so some lowlife could insult him for finishing?" Deep down inside, this just fueled a fire and the announcer is lucky that I didn't knock his lung loose.

As the race went on, I became more aware of the smiles on some of these peoples faces and their desire and happiness to finish the race. I thought to myself, "Crossing that finish line must be an awesome experience." I got to see a dad joined just before the finish line by his two kids who were beaming with pride as they were able to cross the finish line with their dad. I saw a husband wait anxiously for his wife to make the last turn and cross the finish line to receive a big hug. And get this, when you see a seventy-year-old man take on the course and beat guys half his age, that's pretty awesome. The whole day I had noticed that not a single person had made me feel out of place and my perceptions of these elitists were totally wrong.

As the day ended and we loaded up our equipment, I had this feeling that I needed to change, but why did I have this feeling? Was it just because I wanted the attention of crossing the finish line or was it something deeper than that? Whatever it was, I knew that I was going to make a change in my life for fitness, whatever that meant, but where would my drive and motivation come from? Why did I want to do this?

A non-doer is very often a critic-that is, someone who sits back and watches doers, and then waxes philosophically about how the doers are doing. It's easy to be a critic, but being a doer requires effort, risk, and change.
- Dr. Wayne W. Dyer -

A determined soul will do more with a rusty monkey wrench than a loafer will accomplish with all the tools in a machine shop.
- Robert Hughes -

- Chapter Two -
Walking, Jogging…O.K. Slogging!

So I attended my first triathlon as a spectator and I felt as though I needed to change my present level of fitness. I started to question myself with things like what approach will I take? Where will I train? Is this going to cost me anything?

To begin, let me tell you a little bit about myself. Even as a young child, I was overweight, but I never thought that being overweight should keep me from doing something athletic. To this day, I don't know where I got my athletic sense, because my dad really wasn't a big sports fan and had not been involved in sports at all. I was used to hearing comments about how, for my size, I was able to react quickly and was pretty fast. On the other hand, I can remember failing or not being able to do some things because of my size. This really never discouraged me. I just moved on to something else. In high school, I

14

was a power-lifter and in track - throwing the shot put and discus. I really loved to compete. I was always out to show up the little guy or try to be better than anyone could expect. I took great pride in surprising people by doing things they felt that I shouldn't be able to do and it was always fun to be good at something that a "big guy" shouldn't be able to do.

I always had the desire to work hard and if that meant putting in extra time by myself, then that was what I would do. Just to give you an example, in league softball, the most common place to see a big guy is catching behind the plate. Frankly, I was just bored with the thought of being there. So where did I end up? Yep, you guessed it. Being a catcher. I wanted to play in the infield and I told the coach that is where he needed to try to play me. He shrugged me off and said that I was too slow and that I should just stick to catching or riding the bench. Well, he shouldn't have told me that because I was out to prove him wrong and to show him just how little he knew. Every afternoon, I would get home from school and both of my parents would be at work so there were no vehicles under the carport. The back wall of the carport facing the driveway was concrete and made a great backstop. I had found a rubber ball that was about the size of a regulation softball and made out of a material that bounced and reacted much more quickly than softball would. Because the bricks were uneven, the ball would come off the bricks at weird angles. Over the period of a few weeks, I managed to improve my reaction time and moved on to play in the infield.

In college, I decided that none of these sports was going to pay the bills so I parted ways with sports and focused on my education. During college, I worked out with weights, played racquetball, and played a good bit of league softball, so I was able to keep in fairly decent shape. Soon after graduating from college, I went to work and got married so any type of exercise regimen took a back seat to career and spouse.

It was during the next ten years that I began to expand my horizons, which is a nice way of saying I expanded my waist. Oh, don't get me wrong. I went on diets and probably over that ten-year period lost a total of 100 to 150 lbs without exercising, only to see the weight that I lost come back with its own bonus package.

On January 12, 2001, my life underwent a dramatic change with the birth of my son, Christopher Michael Pate. You see, I had said that having a child wouldn't change my life much. My wife and I had been married for ten years before Christopher was born. I was an avid golfer and had worked diligently to break into the low eighties and occasionally into the seventies. Before my son was born, I would spend most evenings at the country club working on my game trying to just take off a couple more strokes. I would go for weeks without missing a day at the country club, even if it was to sneak out for lunch and just practice putting. I'm lucky enough to have a very understanding wife who rarely minded my golf habit.

By now, you are probably starting to pick up on something: I have pretty much an all-or-nothing mentality that can be unhealthy at times. Well, despite my predictions, the birth of my son did change my life and I am not ashamed to admit that I would happily give up time at the golf course to come home and just hold him. During the first sixth months of his life, I began to understand how parents would sacrifice to do anything for their child. I began to realize that this little human being that I held in my arms depended on me to provide, protect and to love him; and, as with anything else, I wanted to be the best father that I could be. But I was also realizing that if I didn't take care of myself, and continued to live a high-risk life due to my physical condition, I would fail. I also knew that even if I was in great physical condition, that if God thought that it was time for Michael Pate to die, I was going to die. Just because I didn't know what tomorrow would hold couldn't be an excuse not to start exercising. In my mind, I knew that my little boy and my wife deserved more from me than the idle lifestyle that I had grown accustomed to.

Okay, now what was I going to do? Well, economically, I felt I couldn't afford to join a gym, and that would knock out swimming and going back to lifting and I didn't have a bicycle, so economically I didn't see this as an option either. I had a pair of tennis shoes. That was it! I would start walking and then I would work up to running.

If you are not familiar with Louisiana in the summer, let me provide you with a little education. It's hot and it's humid. I mean the air sticks to you and some days it feels as thick as syrup when you breathe. It feels as if you could cough and water would shoot from your lungs. Okay, maybe its not quite that bad, but it is so humid that if you haven't been to Louisiana, you just cannot understand. Being the highly educated man that I am, I decided that there is no better time to start running than in the middle of June.

I went out on my first walk on a nice June night when the temperature was about 87 degrees at 9:00 P.M. Now factor in the coefficient of the humidity and it feels like 95 degrees. I made the first 100 yards of my walk and thought, "This is really easy!" At about 110 yards, I started to feel this burning sensation in my shins. By the time I hit the quarter-mile mark, they were really burning. I kept plodding along, hoping that no one was taking their garbage out for the evening. I had convinced myself that if anyone saw me, they would think that I had something wrong with me physically. The further I went, the louder my feet were starting to slap flat against the pavement. I heard dogs barking and babies crying, fearing that "THE END IS NEAR!" as I proceeded through the neighborhood. I finally made it back to my driveway and thought about how pathetic I had become. I couldn't get in a measly half-mile. Being competitive and my own worst critic, I mentally beat myself up for the next twenty-four hours. How could I have been so naive and let myself slip into such a pathetic state of fitness? That night, I even thought about ordering a whole box of the little gadgets that provide electrical stimulation to the muscles and you just sit there and let it do the work. At this point, I didn't care if they made me flop all over my living room. If they worked, it would be worth the investment. Slowly, my brain must have started receiving more oxygen because I realized that this was an absurd way of thinking, but after all I was desperate to start making a change in my life.

Over the next two weeks, things got better and my body didn't seem to be quite as tight as it had been. It was at this point that I decided that walking sucks and I had to move to running. Oh my God, what could I have been thinking? I can't tell you why I thought that I could run, but, hey, I was going to give it a try. At about 100 yards, I thought I was going to blow out a lung. My throat was burning, my eyes were watering and I am sure my lips were turning blue. I could remember doing sprints in high school to work on quickness and remembered that it really hurt, but it had never felt like this! I would walk, then run and so on until I thought I was going to die. To this day, I'll never know how I ever made it back home.

After about three weeks, I could make it about a half-mile without stopping. It was at this point and time I started believing that I could make my come-back. This was encouraging, but during this time, an interesting thing happened to me. While out on one of my nightly adventures, I noticed a truck passed me at a fairly slow pace. Well, that may not seem strange, but a couple of minutes later, the vehicle came by again and I could see an older gentlemen staring at me intently as he came by. A couple of minutes later, the vehicle approached me slowly and this time the driver's side window was down.

As the truck pulled up to me, the elderly man asked, "You need a ride, son?" Now I told him that I didn't but as I looked at him and waddled my way along, in a split second, I wondered what caused the man to stop and ask me if I needed a ride. Did I look like I needed a ride? Did I look so out of place running that he thought that I was in need of rescue?

Then he answered my question, "Son, I just never seen a big feller like you run that fur if he didn't need no help."

Rather than take this as something to be ashamed of, I took it as a compliment. I was doing something that most individuals my size couldn't do. Maybe my way of thinking is totally backwards compared to what it should be, but I was proud that he thought that I must have needed help if I had been running that far.

I did tell some people at work that I had started to run. As this sensitive information was leaked, they began to question me in disbelief. I heard the standard questions: "Don't you think you should see a doctor?" and "Why don't you just get on a diet and loose some weight and then start to exercise?" It was then and there that I realized that they didn't understand that I had started a new personal journey and there was no way they could understand. You will find that people are very uncomfortable as you start to be able to do things that they can't do. They are sometimes placed in a position of guilt because they know that they should start, but just don't know how, and I honestly believe some folks are just hacked off that you as a heavyweight can do more than they can when they are just slightly overweight or out of shape. Be prepared for the criticism and just chalk it up to the fact that they don't know how to handle the aspect that you are doing what you are doing. Most of all, don't let them discourage you. As I pursued my new dream, they just looked at me and said, "Yeah, next month you will be back to the same old you." But this time something seemed different. I had not been this motivated to be athletic for any reason since high school.

Then something awful started happening. My knees would just ache at night and wouldn't stop hurting. I would wake up with them just throbbing and they would get a little better, but then they would start hurting again. I was already losing enough sleep with a seven-month old in the house, but to lose sleep to pain in my knees was just a little too much. I took over-the-counter pain relievers, but it just seemed to get worse. After about two weeks of this, I decided that my knees just weren't up to carrying my large frame around under these conditions. What still baffles me to this very day is the fact that I know I can find either a book or information via the internet that would give me some good basic information about getting started with running. But I didn't choose this route. For the remainder of July and part of August, I just loafed around and my knees seemed to be getting better. I had quit running, but I was determined that this was not going to stop me.

It was then I decided that running was not going to be an option, so where did I go from here? I decided I'd like to ride a bike. That seemed pretty low-impact, but where could I come up with the money to buy a bicycle? In the midst of my new journey, my wife was making a career change that I fully supported, but this put her between paychecks for about three months. Going out and buying a bicycle would not be something that I could do unless I came up with unexpected funds. I searched EBAY. I searched the chain stores and started to try to figure out what kind of bike I would need and what, monetarily, I could spend. It didn't take me long to figure out that I would have to wait until funds were readily available before I would be able to give this serious consideration to a bike of any type.

In the last part of July while attending a conference in Destin, Florida for my company, I received an award. This was not an award with a plaque; it was an award with a check. Now I had the money to go and buy a bicycle, but where would I buy a bicycle? There was so much information on bikes and the rhetoric each company had on their particular bike! It just was confusing. But there was one thing that I knew about my first bike - it would have to hold my big rear end up!

Accepting Award in Destin Florida

Obstacles don't have to stop you.
If you run into a wall,
don't turn around and give up.
Figure out how to climb it,
go through it, or work around it.

–Michael Jordan –

This one step - choosing a goal and sticking to it - changes everything.
- Scott Reed -

- Chapter Three -
I Really, Really, Really Need a Bike!

n Monday morning when I returned from my company trip, the award money that I had received was about to burn a hole in my pocket. I was as excited as a kid on Christmas morning. So many bikes and so little time! I had to get something and get it quick. What should I do about a bike? Should I just go get a bike from a local retailer and pedal away or what?

This is the point when it pays to have friends who will help point you in the right direction. It just happened, I had lunch on that Monday with my friend Brad. After discussing that I thought I would just go on down to the local chain store and pick up a $250.00 mountain bike, I was stopped dead in my tracks.

Brad looked at me with all seriousness and, "Don't go buy a piece of junk just to get a bike to ride." He then started explaining to me that bikes came in sizes. I told him that I knew they came in sizes, some had 20-inch wheels and some had 26-inch wheels, I wasn't stupid. He did agree that bikes came with different size wheels, but informed me that they came with different frame sizes and it would be worth my time to go to the local bike shop to be fitted.

Fitted for a bicycle? This was starting to sound really expensive. He reassured me that if I were properly fitted for a bicycle, I would be more comfortable and would be more likely to stick with it.

After lunch I worked like crazy so I could get out of the office a little early. I drove to the local bike shop and parked right up front. I sucked in my stomach, poked out my chest and walked into the front door of the bike shop. I then asked for the salesperson Brad had told me to speak with. He was a pleasant-looking gentleman, but I had the feeling that he thought I was there to buy a bike for someone else, maybe a birthday present for my kid. Apparently I didn't fit the mold of the typical purchaser of a bike.

"How can I help you?" he asked.

"I need a bicycle for myself," I told him. I'm sure I saw a look of shock flit across his face, but he masked it quickly.

"So what are you looking for?" he asked me when he had recovered.

"Preferably one with two wheels that will go down the road when I pedal it," I said, trying to inject a little humor into this slightly uncomfortable conversation.

He then said, "No, no, no! What type of riding do you plan on doing?"

"The kind where you sit on a seat and move your legs up and down," I said, really not knowing what he wanted from me. By this time, I am sure he realized that he was dealing with a real guru when it comes to bikes.

"Okay, let me ask you this," he says, "What is your goal"?

I had an answer for this. "To get into better shape."

"Do you want a road bike or a mountain bike?"

"I want one with tires that won't go flat when I ride it," I said. "That's what I really want."

He assured me that tires wouldn't be my problem, but how could he be sure of that? He had never stress-tested anything with his 150-pound lean frame. He then showed me some road bikes, but those tires where so small, I figured I would ride about a half-mile and have a flat. Apparently he picked up on my mental block on the tires and we moved to the hybrid bikes. For anyone who doesn't know what a hybrid bike is, this is a cross between a road bike, a comfort bike and a mountain bike. And, oh, the joy that flooded my soul - this one had some big-boy tires on it!

Okay, now we were making some progress. This was a bike I could live with. They didn't have one in stock, but the picture sure did look good. So he showed me some pictures of different bikes and showed me that there were different levels in prices based on the components on the bikes. Now, if you are like I was, you have no idea about what he meant by different components. Components are things like shifters, brakes cranks, and so forth. Just like when you buy a car, you can buy the base-line model or you can pay more for some nicer features or top-of-the-line items. Did I want this or did I want that? What color did I want? Was there a specific tire I was looking for? Would I ride off road? If I did, would it be on a gravel road or would I ride mostly on city streets and through neighborhoods? By the time I walked out of the bike shop, I was starting to get a headache. Finally I decided on a bike in my mind and let the salesman know I wanted that one.

"If this is what you want, then let's get you measured," he said.

What I was picturing was his coming over with a tape measure and measuring my inseam, but here he came with a yardstick-looking device with a wooden dowel sticking out of it. He then stood in front of me and showed me that the dowel slid up and down.

He stood the yardstick up and said, "Now hold the top of the stick and slide the dowel up until it fits snugly against your crotch."

That's what I did, but apparently my definition of snug and his definition of snug just didn't coincide with each other. My definition of snug did not make the pitch of my voice any higher, however his made me feel that I was going to be trying out for the boys choir very soon. So with this pleasant experience out of the way, we were ready to order my bike.

"The Fit Stick"

According to the shop, my bike would take a week to come in, but there was a catch. If my bike didn't come in before Saturday they would be closing the store for vacations and then it would be an additional week before my bike would be there. Then with the delay, it might be another week before I got my bike. Well you guessed it: THREE weeks later, I got my bike.

The day I picked up my bike, I was a little apprehensive. Did I have enough knowledge to ride this fine piece of machinery? So I purchased a computer (which is a glorified electronic speedometer) for my bike and a helmet and waited patiently as they brought my new toy out from the back of the store. My first bike. I was like a new dad getting to see his child for the first time. Suddenly I noticed a defect with my bike. Apparently they had put my seat on someone else's bike. They couldn't expect me to sit on that little seat! It would disappear when I sat on it! Where is the comfort part of the bike? The seat was supposed to be comfortable, right? It must have been really apparent that I had concern in my eyes about the seat, because I was assured that we could change it out for another seat. Of course, that would cost a little more. The nice salesman told me to give it a try and it would be better than I thought. Well, okay, you pencil-neck, I'll try it.

I took my bike home, put on my helmet and off I went. I must admit that I had the perfect place to start riding. It just so happens that I live next to the entrance of a subdivision that has an outer street, which follows the parameter of the neighborhood and ends up being a 1.5-mile loop. The great thing about this neighborhood is the fact that there is no through traffic, so that eliminates one of my major concerns. I was off like a speeding bullet – well, not exactly, but I felt good about this ride. I rode 1.5 miles without stopping, which had to count for something. The seat didn't hurt my backside as much as I thought it would, but I have to say that some of those big wide seats that look like they should be on a lawn tractor would have been really comfortable.

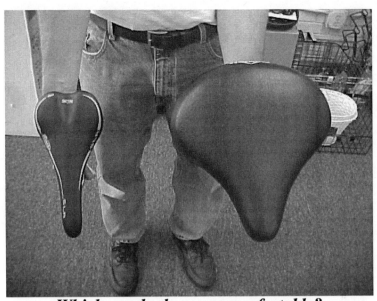

Which one looks more comfortable?

Since I had the option of riding at night in a well-lit neighborhood, and since it would, after all, be cooler, I decided that I needed to ride every day. So the next evening I got on the bike at about 8:30 and as I sat down on the seat, a pain shot up from my backside straight to my brain. It was then and there that I adopted the saying, "The brain says go but the butt says no." In a way, this ended up being a good thing. I rode for the next two weeks, only putting in a mile and a half. What I didn't realize was that I was starting to build a base (this is just my way of saying that I was strengthening my muscles, lungs, and heart) and good old backside calluses.

After a couple of weeks I moved up to three miles and let my body adjust to that distance and the time on the seat. Over time, I began to progress and after a couple months, I had worked up to making a nine-mile ride. Even though I had tried to let my backside adjust to the seat, I still was experiencing discomfort and that was really starting to get old. One of my friends suggested that I buy a pair of bike shorts. What a suggestion! I would look really good in those! But I was tired of being sore and if this was the answer, I would give it a try. So I made the big purchase from the local bike shop - they carried big boy sizes. I went home and tried them on and decided that since I was riding at night, maybe this would make it better. After about six miles, I decided that it really didn't matter what I looked like, because this made things all better. Also during this time, one of my friends decided that he would buy a comfort bike and he started joining me on the Tour de Neighborhood which gave me some accountability and kept me riding. As my rides progressed and began getting longer, I had begun to have pressure and pain in my hands, but despite the pain, I pressed on. I was faithful for the next months and was starting to feel really comfortable on my bike.

Around this time, a couple of my friends, Jay and Jeff, who are triathletes, asked me to go on a short flat ride with them, so I agreed. I met them on a cool morning in October and immediately was intimidated just from looking at their bikes and the way they dressed. Even if they didn't ride fast, they just looked fast. So off I went, preparing to chase these veterans through the winding flat roads and not really knowing what to expect. Surprisingly, I was able to keep up. This was their slow flat recovery ride, but I did keep up for the 11.2 miles, which was a new personal best. I have to say that this was my first milestone. These guys were really encouraging and pumped me up about the condition that I was in. When you are a big guy and the little guys think you are doing well, then you get a little excited.

One thing that my friends noticed was that I was riding with my seat just a little low and they thought that I would gain much improvement from buying cycling shoes and pedals. Things quickly went into high gear because Jay thought that he had a pair of pedals that he would swap me out for lunch. Now all I needed was the shoes. Well, I found a pair of, get this, *tri shoes*, on clearance on the Internet. Even though I really hadn't locked into the idea of doing any type of triathlon at the time, I liked them because they didn't lace up, they just had a Velcro strap on them so they were quick to get in and out of. I got the pedals on my bike, the clips on my shoes and I was ready to give it a try. Now I am the same guy who just a few months ago thought that you were a couple of fries short of a Happy Meal if you were permanently attaching yourself to a bicycle.

The next week, I got a call about going on a ride with them again and it was a short ride that was flat and about the same distance. This seemed to be the perfect way to try out this new clipped-in method that was supposed to make me more efficient. I had, for the last week, tweaked the pedals to a point at which I thought that I was comfortable with them. So I showed up and told Jay that I was really excited about the pedals and how they were making me feel one with the bike. I told him that I was going to ride up the road about twenty yards just to make sure that I was comfortable with them. As I pulled back up to Jay, I kicked out my left foot as I slowed and for some unknown reason, I leaned to the right, which was the side that was still clipped in. It took forever for me to finally hit the ground, but my right foot came unclipped. As a matter of fact, I unclipped my butt, my teeth, my everything. I was assured that this happened to everyone at sometime, but that didn't make me feel any better. At least it was out of the way and hopefully it wouldn't happen again. After I hit the pavement, I made an assessment of my bike and myself and all seemed well.

After we were into the ride about six miles, one of the guys said, "You've got blood running down from your knee."

Being the ever-aggressive "Rambo of the Bike,"I glanced down and assured him, "It's just a scratch - makes you tougher!"

My riding continued to improve and I was able to make a 16.2-mile ride in the first of December and my time was 1 hour and 8 minutes. What was encouraging was that this was a pretty hilly ride and the ride out was into a headwind. Don't get me wrong, this was a really tough ride to me. I went to a crawl on some of the hills, but I kept plodding along. Jeff and Jay were riding with me and were giving me the courtesy of hanging back giving me moral support instead of running off and leaving me. I was really starting to feel good about what I was accomplishing and felt I was on the right track. By this time of the year temperatures were starting to drop below 50 degrees and I really didn't want to make an investment in winter gear to ride in. On the other hand, I didn't want to quit either. Rides were harder to get in, but I still rode when I could, going into a mode of maintaining the base that I had built.

In the latter part of December while on a ride, Jay planted the seed that there would be a training series of sprint triathlons that the local tri club would put on. I knew that this would mean that I had to rethink my training and move to a more rounded training regimen, which would include swimming and starting to run in addition to biking.

It's not what I did today - it's what I know I can do tomorrow.
- Michael Pate -

Every worthwhile accomplishment, big or little, has its stages of drudgery and triumph; a beginning, a struggle and a victory.
- Ghandi -

- Chapter Four -
The Lost Art of Swimming!

oving to a more rounded training regimen included something that I wasn't really sure about and that was swimming. Sure I could swim, but not in the athletic sense. I was comfortable in the water and through high school and college spent a great deal of time on the lake in the old ski boat. I didn't think I had a fear of the water, but I had a fear of being accepted wherever I decided to swim. Now I knew that I wouldn't be running down to the local sporting goods store and getting a Speedo bathing suit with my current physique and when it came down to it I was sure there were rules about what I would be allowed to swim in. In a Speedo, I am sure that we would have had reported sightings of Bigfoot and, before you ask, no I my body is not covered in hair. I just don't think that it would have been a pleasant experience for the other patrons of the pool. I now had to find a place to swim.

Since it was cool weather, I only had two options when it came to places to swim: either I went to the local YMCA or I would go to the Louisiana Athletic Club on the campus of Louisiana College. After weighing both options, the biggest factor that I would have was time. For one thing, I had vowed to myself that I would not let training interfere with several things listed in this order: GOD, family, or work. I had vowed not to let training interfere with me going to church on Sunday or Wednesday nights, which hadn't been a problem so I was off to a good start. My wife is a teacher and leaves every morning for work at 6:30 so I would have to work around that. I tried to be at the office between 7:00 and 7:30 every morning. Since the YMCA was fairly close and was cheaper than my other alternative, I chose the Y.

On January 2, 2002 I joined our local Y and vowed to start swimming. I would have to swim and be out of the water by 6:05 in order to race back home, take a shower and get ready to take my son to daycare by 6:30. It could be done and it would take some sacrifice on my part, but it was worth it. If I was going to do a triathlon in the early Spring, I had to start now. A couple of days later, I had figured it out: I would arrive at the Y at 5:30 am and could get in my swim and be back at home and ready to go to leave by 6:30 am. This might sound trivial, but at that time of the morning the traffic lights were timed perfectly if I drove at just the right speed I would never have to stop until a stop sign one block from my house.

As with biking, I had no clue about swimming. I arrived at the Y the first morning ready to start a new adventure.

As I walked in, the lady at the desk said, "You can't swim without a towel."

I had it when I left, or did I? I raced back out to my vehicle and, to my surprise, there was no towel.

So I went back in and asked the nice lady "Can I swim if I dry off with my t-shirt? After all, it's bigger than a beach towel."

Now by this time in the journey I had dropped about 15 pounds and was feeling a good bit better about my level of fitness, but this whole taking your shirt off to swim was what I was really nervous about. So off the shirt came and with lighting speed I was in the pool. Okay, I am in the pool and I had to decide how would I look the coolest. I remembered that in the Summer Olympics the swimmers flapped their arms back and forth so I would do this to warm up. So I started flapping my arms and I flapped for about a minute. Okay, it might have only been thirty seconds, but maybe it made me look good and like I knew what I was doing.

Then I began my pep talk. *Okay I am going to do this. That water looks deep on the other end, but there's a life guard so I should be okay, RIGHT?!* So I took off doing the freestyle/crawl stroke and the first twenty-five yards wasn't too bad. On the way back, I started to feel a little fatigue, but I could do this! This was only a total of 50 yards. On the way back down the pool, I caught a glimpse of something that was quite disturbing. It was the lifeguard and she had a look of fear. She was downright scared. She was afraid that she was going to have to save me. I swear, as I made the turn to come back to make a hundred yards, I too thought that she was going to have to save me. My heart was about to beat out of my chest. Not only did I have that sinking feeling in my chest, I really was sinking! I kicked harder and pulled harder but the wall just wasn't getting any closer. Finally, I reached the shallow end of the pool and walked the last ten yards.

As I got out of the pool, I looked around and there was a little old man making his way up and down the first lane. In lane two, there was a gentleman who was swimming and looked as if he knew what he was doing and seemed pretty fast. In next lane was an elderly gentlemen doing the sidestroke and just floating in the pool was another gentlemen with a pool noodle wrapped around his chest. I walked out from the Y that morning defeated because I felt that I didn't belong there and didn't have a clue as to what I was really supposed to do.

Later that day at work, still feeling defeated, but not depressed the phone rang and it was Jay. As I answered the line, the first words out of his mouth were, "So how did your swim go?"

I didn't want to tell him that I was defeated before I could even make it a hundred yards, but this was Jay and he was my friend, so I told him.

He didn't laugh at me. He didn't say anything negative. He just said, "That's good."

I expressed to him my disappointment and he reassured me that things would get better - I just had to keep trying. This was just what I needed. That night, I went home and started to read about swimming and what it really entailed as a form of exercise. I realized from my little bit of research that I would have to build a base just like I did on the bike and it would get better over time. I decided that I would use the backstroke since I thought it would be easier to do and seemed fairly simple. That same night I started to focus on what my goal was and that was to be able to do a triathlon. Like I have said before, this was a different feeling than I had ever been in touch with.

Over the next couple of weeks, I tried to get in just a hundred yards without dying and things started to get better. As I continued to swim, I noticed that everybody wasn't doing some fancy stroke, some folks were just getting from one end of the pool to the other. However, they were putting in the time. Soon I changed to the sidestroke and started to try to become a little faster.

Something started happening to me. As I tried to swim harder, I began to have a restricted feeling in my chest and would get really short of breath. It would get so bad that I would stand up before I was to the end of a lap.

What was strange was that as soon as I stood up, it would go away. I must admit I thought that something was physically wrong with me. Did I have heart or lung problems?

So one day at lunch I told Jay what was happening and he immediately had a concerned look. However, when I told him that I would stand up and it was okay, he just smiled and said, "Why don't you try to relax the next time it happens."

Well, I did, and sure enough, I was not relaxing and was almost panicking and that was causing my problem.

NEWS FLASH, NEWS FLASH If you are reading this and have problems such as this, don't treat them lightly due to the fact that it could be a serious health problem!

Even as I improved, I was still slow. The thing that just got me so aggravated was that a 60-year old man just kept lapping me and that just made me mad. I was burning up the pool and only able to do 200 yards in 12 minutes. What I did realize was that I needed to get someone to help me and with the amount of friends that I had around me that were good swimmers, I was confident that one of them would help me.

Just as a side note, and this may not be the real reason this happened, but you remember the lifeguard who had that fearful look on her face? She quit after I had been swimming about three weeks. I guess she just couldn't handle the fact that she might have to pull me out of the water. She probably didn't sleep at night and she probably just woke up in a cold sweat when she did sleep. She should have stayed though. She could have seen the comeback.

In reading the lives of great men, I found that the first victory they won was over themselves... self-discipline with all of them came first.
- Harry S. Truman -

Even when opportunity knocks,
a man still has to get up off his seat
and open the door.
- Anonymous -

- Chapter Five -
A Little Coaching Goes A Long Way

If you are overweight, it can be a major challenge just to ask someone to help you or to ask them to work out with you. So asking someone to give me a little advice on swimming was not that easy for me. Fortunately, my friend Jay had taught swimming and was more than willing to give me some assistance. At times like these, you see who your real friends are. Jay was willing to get up and meet me at the pool at 5:30 in the morning and wasn't getting anything in return for it.

Early one morning in late January we met at the pool and Jay told me to do a warm up lap or two. I thought I would impress him with my backstroke. I blazed down the pool and back - at least, in my mind I was blazing –and was ready to start a little poolside instruction. Surely after Jay saw that I was doing my backstroke so well, he would be impressed. But I had asked him to help me with the freestyle stroke, specifically starting to swim with my face in the water.

If you have read anything about swimming, you have probably noticed that people talk about efficiency in the water. If you are swimming with your head out of the water, this makes you less efficient because if your head is up, your legs and feet will be pointed down and this creates more drag. And let's face it, when you already are dragging your big body through the water, you don't need any more drag than you already have.

What inspiring bit of information would Jay give me? First, he told me to just push off from the end of the pool and glide until I stopped, keeping my face underwater. Okay, this wasn't too bad. We repeated this about 10 times. Next he told me to do the same thing, but to start trying to swim the crawl/freestyle stroke. (Yeah, he did tell me some other technical things, but this is not a how-to-swim book!).

This is where things started getting difficult. I would make about two strokes - three at the most - and would swallow water. Twenty minutes later, I had swallowed so much water that I was beginning to get sick. I couldn't fathom that this would ever get any better.

I struggled back to the end of the pool and asked Jay this simple question, "How long will it take to get better?"

With all sincerity, he answered, "About two weeks."

Two weeks. I could live with that. I could suffer through anything for two weeks.

At the end of two weeks, things weren't any better. I couldn't get from one end of the pool the other without stopping because I was swallowing so much water. After two more weeks, I did see some improvement, but this was just starting to get downright discouraging. I felt that I had digressed from the first day that I was in the pool. However, I just had a determination that I would keep

43

trying and it would get better. After about two months, it was better and I could go from one end of the pool to the other without stopping. Then I was able to make it 200 yards, 300 yards, 800 yards, and then one day, I went to the pool and put in a total of 1300 yards! Swimming was becoming more of a natural activity, and, as with anything, when you start to improve, you gain confidence and encouragement.

Every Monday, Wednesday, and Friday, I faithfully got up and went to the pool and would swim specifically concentrating on my stroke. I would time myself and just couldn't seem to make it up to the speed of the other swimmers. What was I doing wrong? What could I do to get better? Was I just destined to be a super slow swimmer? One day at lunch, I was whining to my friend Brad when he reminded me that I shouldn't be worrying about speed. I should just be concentrating on getting out of the water if I wanted to do a triathlon. You see, I tend to lose focus on what my immediate goal should be and my goal, honestly, was to finish. I had gotten lost in the fact that I wasn't fast enough in my mind.

One thing that had made my effort more bearable was that I did have friend who had joined the Y right after I did. He had been swimming in the lane beside me for the last few months. That friend was Jeff - the same Jeff who had been one of the people who had encouraged me on the bike. Even though his training method was not the same as mine and he was much faster, we did have some accountability to each other and it's nice to have someone there to encourage you. It takes special people like Jeff encouraging you to keep going. Sometimes you are improving even when you don't realize it. A good training partner can help you keep your head up and keep going.

Just a little word of wisdom, if you are going to start training for a triathlon, don't make the mistake of thinking that whatever distance you have to swim is easy. Make the sacrifice and get in the pool and work on your swim. Your chances of getting in trouble on the swim are greater than any other event in a triathlon. Get someone to help you with the basics of the swim stroke from the beginning. In my opinion, I would have been much better off to have some basic instruction from the beginning, rather than aimlessly splashing around for a month in the pool. I know now that learning to be efficient in the water is a very important part of the swim and if you don't have the stroke down, you are wasting unnecessary energy.

Make it your goal to be the most dedicated and consistent swimmer at whatever pool you go to. I will tell you right now that there are going to be some individuals who will be there every time you're there and rest assured they will be there when you're not, so strive to be most dedicated person at the pool. Over time, you will grow to know these people and when you return after being out for a while, they will tell you they have missed you. There will be elderly people. There will be young people. There will be men. There will be women. There will be people from every imaginable walk of life at the pool.

There is a little fellow who swims everyday at the Y, and he is there when I get there and he is there when I leave. I probably swim twice as fast as he does, but this little old man has taught me one thing. It doesn't matter how fast you are and how good you look. What matters is that you are consistently making an effort to better yourself. I have to admit that it is nice to hear that little ole' fella say good morning and wish me a great day. Even if I miss a day or choose to swim at a different time, it is nice to hear him say, "We've been missing you!"

Whatever you decide to do - find a coach or go at it alone- dedicate yourself to learning the basics of the swim and becoming confident in your swimming ability. It may take you a week, a month or a year, but with persistence, you can develop your swim into a confident part of your workout and training schedule.

Ability is what you're capable of doing. Motivation determines what you do. Attitude determines how well you do it.
- Lou Holtz -

The horizon is out there somewhere,
and you just keep chasing it, looking
for it, and working for it.
- Bob Dole -

- Chapter Six -
I'm Ready to Tri It Naked

The week before my first sprint triathlon was anything but usual. My friends, who in my mind were – and still are - very accomplished athletes, had convinced me to join the local tri club. Now if you are reading this and you are a Clydesdale or Athena, joining a tri club and going to the first meeting is not something you look forward to. At my first meeting, I tried to time it so that I was not early since I didn't want people to ask me any questions. The other thing was that the meeting was held at a local restaurant owned by one of the local tri club members. The meeting was held there because the restaurant is closed on Monday evenings and I was sure if I walked up late to the meeting that someone was going to tell me that they were closed and this was a private meeting. As with most triathlon things so far, I was prepared for some type of situation that would make me feel uncomfortable.

I had this whole time thing mapped and down to an exact science. I would arrive about one minute before the meeting started and walk in with only seconds to spare. As with most well-laid, good-intentioned plans, things didn't exactly happen the way I'd hoped. I arrived with one minute to spare only to walk up and realize that the owner of the restaurant had not shown up and everyone was standing outside waiting on him. What made it even worse was that none of my friends had shown up yet. This group of athletes would surely stare at me and wonder what I was doing at a meeting for their tri club. But just the opposite happened. They started treating me just like I was one of them and they didn't seem to see me in any different light than anyone else. They weren't worried about my physical make-up, just the fact that I apparently had somewhere deep down inside the same burning desire to compete, not with them, but with myself. I walked away from that meeting with a little more confidence. I had thought that I would walk in and would have them shun me to some corner reserved for rejects who didn't fit their idea of fitness. Instead, I walked out with a new set of friends.

As the days of the week passed, I had convinced myself that I had prepared the best that I was capable of. I was on the final countdown and I have to admit that I was getting scared and my nerves were starting to get the best of me. I had tried to figure out what to do for my transition area and how I would set it up. I had tried to visualize the swim, bike, and the RUN. I had given myself pep talks about how I could do this and I just needed to race my own race and race to finish. Even though I was racing to finish, I had a goal of getting through in 1 hour 30 minutes.

Friday evening tolled around and my wife's obsessive list-making had rubbed off on me. I had made a list of everything that I needed for the triathlon. Unlike my wife, I had not written it in grammatically correct outline form, but I had it divided into categories of swim, bike, and run. At about 8:30, I started preparing to load my gear for the next morning and all seemed to be going well. Almost too well.

As I started to move my bike, I noticed what seemed to be a low tire. It wasn't low, it was flat. In a panic, I raced to get my bike pump to inflate the tire. I pumped like a madman trying to air up that tire but it just wouldn't hold air.

Immediately, I started pacing through the house, and I have to be honest, I just wanted to cry, I didn't have a spare tube for my tire and didn't have a clue as to what I would do. I felt like a train that had been climbing a long hill and just as I came over the crest of the hill, I realized I had no brakes and I was descending out of control.

I thought about going to the local retail chain, but I didn't have a clue as to what size tube I would need and had a feeling that they wouldn't either.

My wife tried to calm me while I paced. She suggested, "Why don't you call the local bike shop owner."

I told her – almost hysterically "The shop is closed!"

She very calmly asked, "Can you call him at home?"

"At home? How could I call him at home? I don't even know his number!"

She patiently asked me his name and then found the number in the phone book and even dialed it for me.

I shifted my weight from one foot to the other while it rang and then one of his kids answered "Hellooooo?"

I asked, "Can I speak to Mike?" and when he picked up the phone, I told him my plight. I'm sure that I was talking so fast and in such a panicked tone that he thought I had lost my mind, but he listened quietly while I asked him where to get a tube at this late hour. I told him that I had been hesitant about calling him because I hate when people call me at home about work and usually wouldn't even think about doing this, but I was REALLY desperate. My wife watched in silence and patted my leg a few times to try to reassure me that everything would be fine, but I just kept thinking that I had trained so hard just to do this short little sprint and now it was all falling apart.

In a calm voice – the kind you use when cornered by a crazed wild animal - he said, "I have a young man working late at the shop putting bikes together and if you'll go straight to the bike shop, he'll probably still be there."

Before I could ask my next question, he answered it by saying "If he has already left, just call back and I will get you taken care of."

Let's stop for a quick message:
Your local bike shop: you know, the one where they have all the nice bikes? If you have a bike shop that is willing to help you out and get you out of a bind, then you need to do business with them. If you don't have a local bike shop, then you might have to do mail order, but you can't get the help I got from a mail order or Internet company.

So anyway, to shorten this story, I went to the bike shop ended up with my flat fixed and was calmed considerably from where I had been only thirty minutes before.

That night I hardly slept at all. I was nervous about the swim, and kept trying to visualize each event. I wasn't trying to visualize the course for each event but I tried to coach myself about being relaxed and finding my own pace. I have an all-or-nothing personality that sometimes hinders me in any type of competition, so I thought it was worth my time to think about my pace and finishing. I even tried to visualize driving into the venue and what that would be like just trying to be relaxed about the unknown.

After lying in bed awake most of the night, I finally heard the alarm go off at 4:30 a.m.

Getting up, I took a quick shower and ate some oatmeal and drank a glass of juice. I began to double-check to make sure all my gear was where it was supposed to be and it seemed that I had done a pretty good job of putting it together. Part of my strategy was not to get in a rush and to remain calm and relaxed without any rushing around at the last minute. I was ready in enough time that I was able to sit down in the recliner and watch a little news before it was time to leave. This venue was only twenty minutes away so I planned on leaving at about 6:30 a.m.

As I arrived at the venue, there were several other people waiting to go into the area of the park where it would be held. It turned out the gate was locked and wouldn't be open for at least another 15 minutes. All my visualization about what to expect was shot out the window.

The gate was finally unlocked and we were ready to move down to the transition area. I quickly set up my transition area and double-checked everything. It all seemed to be in place and where I needed it, but what did I know? This was the first time that I had tried this.

My friends came up to me and reassured me that I was going to do fine. "Just focus on finishing" and I would be all right.

This did help my nerves some, but I still had a lot of fear and anxiety deep down in the pit of my stomach. Sure, it could have just been that oatmeal, but I was ready to just get the show on the road.

My wife arrived with our son and she strolled him over to wish me luck. I was a little distracted and don't remember a word she said. I think I may have even pretty much ignored them, but I was glad they were there. There weren't very many spectators there since this was a training series, but I was happy that they had come.

There would only be one wave for the start and it would be an open deep-water start. As I entered the water and got about waist deep, I swam a few strokes toward the starting area and it felt okay.

Looking back, this is where I started making my first mistakes. I – Mr. Competitive - jumped up right in the middle of everybody for the start. When the whistle blew, the water started churning and I started to make my first stroke when I saw a foot kick to the right of my face. I started feeling as if I had never been swimming before in my life. I would try to swim a few strokes but the whole breathing thing just wasn't working out that well for me. After about 25 yards, I decided it was time to go into survival mode and just do the sidestroke. I started having visions of that little old man passing me in the pool and how embarrassing it was to be doing the sidestroke.

This is a good time to give you some free advice. I don't care how many times you have been in the open water. When you start swimming the freestyle and the water is dirty and you get kicked or realize there are no lines on the bottom of the lake to keep you going straight, you have a tendency to panic. Later, I had the good fortune of speaking with a local psychologist concerning this and it did make me feel better to know that many triathletes suffer from the same panicking feeling even after years of triathlons. I would advise you to try to make some type of open water swim in advance. Just get a few of your training partners and go to the lake and swim from buoy to buoy in the swim area.

I only had to go out a hundred yards and come back, but it seemed I was never going to get to the turnaround marker. Finally, I did make it out of the water and was fairly upset with myself due to what I considered to be a super-slow performance on the swim. As I made it to the transition area, I wasn't that tired but tried to speed up and this just caused me to get aggravated when my shirt started sticking to my wet body and didn't want to go on. I was so disgusted with myself that I didn't speak to my wife or even look in her direction. By the time I mounted the bike and got started, I was fuming. I made my way out onto the route and began pushing myself harder than I should have. About a mile into the bike ride, there is a downhill section that is about ½ mile long. By the time I got to it, I needed a downhill section. The rest of the course was pretty flat, so I started making up some ground. As I made it to the turnaround and started back, my bike computer was ticking along and I was faster than I had anticipated by about two minutes. This gave me some much-needed encouragement, and it seemed that some of my fatigue and frustration disappeared. As I pedaled, I began to reflect on that nice long downhill. That downhill was going to be an uphill and I then realized that all those flat rides I had made were going to be rendered useless. I turned the corner coming into the park entrance and there it was staring me in the face: MT. EVEREST. I started pedaling and up that hill I went. At times I was really getting aggravated about how slow I was going up the hill, but as long as I kept going, the end would soon be in sight.

As I came into the entrance of the park there were some of those fast little guys already at the turn around on the run. Don't you just love to hate those guys? I barreled on to the end of the bike leg and ended up with a fairly decent time for myself.

As I came into the transition area, my wife said in shock, "Oh, no, you had a wreck and you are bleeding!"

I hadn't had a wreck, but she pointed at the back of my bike jersey and down my leg there was a substance that looked just like blood. It wasn't blood. It was my energy gel that had leaked and ran down my leg. I had purchased a chocolate energy gel and it came with a flask. I don't know if I didn't close the cap properly on the flask or if it was defective, but it had leaked in the back pocket of my bike shirt and run down my leg. After the race, my good friend John said that he had seen the brown stuff running down my leg and had just thought I was giving it all I had and didn't stop to use the bathroom. I'm competitive, but I would have stopped to go to the bathroom

I just happened to have a t-shirt that I had worn on the way to the venue, so I was able to change, get cleaned up and head out on the run. Even doing brick workouts (a brick workout is a training exercise in which you perform two of the events back to back and most of the time it is a bike/run) had not prepared me for this. I just couldn't get my legs to move. I had pedaled a little too hard and my legs were just not listening to my brain. I will admit that I walked a majority of the run, but I just kept going and moving on. I must have been walking pretty slowly at times, because at one time a lady pulled up beside me and started trying to ask me directions. In my most polite "LEAVE ME ALONE" voice, I informed her that I didn't have a clue. As I got about 300 yards from the finish line, I realized that I was going to finish this race. Now this race wasn't a big deal for a lot of the people, but it was for me. I had worked more for this than anything that I could remember in the last 15 years. I had made sacrifices in order to train and it was finally paying off. I have to admit, I had to fight back tears the closer I got to the finish line. I was about to accomplish a goal that was beneficial for my family, not for a multimillion-dollar company, not to impress anybody, but just for my family and me. In some weird way, I didn't want to cross the finish line, because I was scared that the feeling of accomplishment would somehow disappear. As I finally slogged across the finish line, several of my friends had waited around for me. I received a host of high fives and compliments but their support and friendship was worth more than a medal or a ribbon. I had done something that had seemed unattainable a year before, but this was only the start. You see to everyone else, this little sprint early in the tri-season was just a short little time of training. For me, it was the start of what I wanted my life to change into.

My time on my first triathlon was one-hour twenty-four minutes and some change. The Tri Club had put together a shirt for the training series and I was originally told that if you finished all three of the training triathlons, you could purchase a shirt. The name of this series was called TRI IT NAKED and had a neat logo design that was sure to attract attention if you wore it in public. After the first race, one of the organizers called me and said that he had my shirt at his office and to run by and pick it up, so I did. Having this shirt was supposed to mean that you finished all three races. Then and there, I vowed to myself that I would not wear the shirt or even try it on if I didn't complete all three. You see, this may sound trivial to you, but I never wanted anyone to question whether I really earned that shirt. I wanted to say to myself that I was able to complete the task and if I did, there would be no doubt that I deserved the shirt.

Great things are not done by impulse,
but by a series of small things brought
together.
- Vincent Van Gogh -

Goals. There's no telling what you can do when you get inspired by them. There's no telling what you can do when you believe in them. There's no telling what will happen when you act upon them.
- Jim Rohn -

- Chapter 7 -
I Want to Go Faster Than a Snail!

eedless to say, after my first sprint, I started to analyze where I was losing time and what I needed to do to improve. I knew that I would do a lot better if I didn't panic on the swim and if I could improve on the run. Another interesting turn of events had come about. When my wife was at my first sprint, she saw that I was pretty serious about this and that my bike was very obviously different from everyone else's. So that evening we had discussed the possible purchase of a new bike. I knew that with a new bike, I probably could reduce my bike time.

While I was happy about the prospect of a new bike, I had learned that when it came to swimming, even after educating myself, I was no better off than when I started. Sure I had gotten a little better, but I still wasn't swimming as quickly as I had hoped and really was at a point where I didn't know what to do to improve. Then one day, I was swimming in a lane next to a gentleman named Steve who was an attorney and currently clerking for a judge in our city. I had asked Steve some basic questions and he had been more than happy to assist me in the past. During our conversation, he had said some nice, encouraging words to me about how much progress I had made; I told him that I was at the end of my rope and didn't know what to do next. Then Steve did one of the nicest things: he offered to meet with me on Wednesday mornings and said he would not swim but just work with me and try to help me improve. He said that he would just move one of his swim days to the weekend and coach me. After three months of swimming in the pool with me, he had gained my respect and I knew that he was a pretty fast swimmer, so I felt that anything that he could share with me would be valuable. So I started meeting him on Wednesdays.

On the first Wednesday that he met with me, he started getting me to work on some different drills and then he hit me with a biggie at the end: I was going to swim intervals. He told me to give it all I had and swim a lap and he would time me. I swam that lap as hard as I could without getting out of control and, as I expected, it was pretty slow - one minute, thirty-seven seconds. Steve told me that we were going to swim a total of 200 yards and that we were going to swim 50-yard intervals with 15 seconds of rest. I didn't have a clue why we were doing this, but if I was going to get any better, I was willing to give it a try.

When we got to the last fifty yards, I was about to throw up. I was sick and didn't want to do anything but leave the pool, go home and puke my guts out. I must say that by the time I arrived back at home I was feeling much better and believed that this had to help me improve just because I was exercising at a level that I had not previously attained. In my mind, it was comparable to being in the midst of a raging storm. During the storm it seems really bad, but after the storm passes, it usually isn't as bad as it seemed.

After about three weeks, I had taken about ten seconds off my fifty-yard time and was starting to see improvements. Steve had helped me develop a workout and I was sticking to it. Now, don't get me wrong - I still knew that I wasn't a speedster in the pool, but I was seeing some improvement. So with Steve's workout program, I was gaining confidence and decreasing my lap times. I had also made a couple of open-water swims to try to alleviate any panic that I might have on race day. The open water swims were a real benefit because they allowed me to do some training other than at the start of a race.

On one of our Sunday afternoon swims, a group of people from our tri club met and we decided that we were all going to swim and some of them would go on and do a bike and run also. So we eased out into the water and moved out to the buoys and started to swim the normal course that was used for the first sprint. A couple of us just wanted to do a swim of 200 yards out and back. So off we went. We estimated where the 200-yard mark would be and we made our return. I had been told that the Tri Club had permission to swim out past the buoys so I didn't think anything about it. As we came onto the beach area, there was a park ranger waiting who informed us that we were not to swim past the swim markers 25 yards off the beach. OOPS! You should have seen the look on his face. After all, this was a lot of excitement for a Sunday afternoon. To him this had to be like someone getting in a barrel and going over the edge at Niagara Falls. Why in the world would someone want to swim out past the buoys anyway? We tried to explain to him that we were supposed to have permission, but on a Sunday afternoon, of course, the guy who had given us permission was not there, so we apologized for any trouble we caused and promised not to do it again until next time. The reality of the situation was that he was doing his job and we had to respect him for that.

I started doing some running and trying to decrease my time, but I just had not spent the time building the base that I should have. When I analyzed my training, I had spent more time in the pool and on the bike and it showed on the run. So I started an interval program of walking and running. I started out with less than I could do, but wanted to try to improve without causing injury. It was slow going, but I vowed to keep plugging away and surely it would improve. I know that the impact that my body weight had on my run made me miserable, but it was getting better. I still was doing more than the last time I tried this whole running bit. And so far, I had not suffered any knee pain and that was really encouraging. This could have been partly because I had lost about eighteen pounds.

Well, as I mentioned before, my wife was starting to realize that I was getting serious about this whole training deal. She had become aware that I was riding a bike that was just nothing compared to what even a road bike would be. In our discussion, she had said that if I were really serious and I went ahead and dropped my membership to the country club, that we could handle me buying a new bike. I also would have a golf cart that really would be of no use so I could sell it and that would go toward my new bike. How I had gotten to the point where I had forgotten about GOLF, I really couldn't tell you. The sport that had once consumed me was something that I rarely even thought about anymore. I had even cancelled my subscription to my golf magazine. Holy Smoke! What was I becoming? I was willing to sell my golf cart to get money for a bike!

What kind of bike would I get? Well, if you haven't figured it out by what you have already read, I always try to gain as much knowledge as I can to make an educated decision. I looked at the Softrides, Treks, and

Cannondales, and just kept feeling like I was not finding the bike that would meet my needs.

I really had heard good things about Softrides, but to be suspended on a beam over the rear tire was a concern for me as a big guy. Every dealer I called assured me that they had big guys on these bikes, and weight wasn't a problem. I called the factory and was told that because of my weight I would void the warranty, but they would sell me new parts at 40% off the price. My concern was if they didn't offer a warranty on the beam because of my weight, then they must have some concern about the beam collapsing. Now, I am no rocket scientist, and don't know what would happen if the beam broke on that bike, but it seemed it would be less painful to just go to the doctor's office and have the vasectomy there.

Disclaimer: I'm in no way saying that there is a problem with the engineering of a Softride bike, nor that the beam would actually break and cause injury to the rider. This is just an expression of my own ignorance about what I was scared would happen to me. Please call Softride with any questions you may have concerning their bikes.

Photo courtesy of Softride

After investigating other possibilities, I just didn't have faith in the information that I was getting. That was when my friend Brad (he was the race director for Indian Creek Triathlon) told me to give his friend BoBo a call. I had only met BoBo one other time, but he was or had been a pro-triathlete with a few sponsors. His website address is **www.bobozone.com** and that's where I got his phone number. I gave him a call and described to him who I was, stressing that I was concerned about my weight and the stress it would place on the frame of a bike and what my big butt would do to those little tires. I spent a great deal of time on the phone with him getting some good advice. This guy sells bikes, yet he told me from the beginning that if my local bike shop would give me support at a competitive price, I should do business with them.

He steered me toward looking at a bike with a composite frame and I specifically moved toward a Kestrel Talon. He informed me of what price he could sell it for on a mail order basis and I have to admit that it was a good deal. I still felt, however, that I owed it to my local bike shop to at least give them a chance to give me a price. I was surprised that the local bike shop agreed to sell the bike within a hundred dollars of what I could get it for if I mail ordered it. Since the owner of the local bike shop had bailed me out in the midst of my panic attack the night before the first sprint, I just couldn't see not buying it from him. When it arrived at the bike shop, boy, was she a beauty. One of the neat things was that I just happened to be in the shop when my bike arrived and I was able to open the box and was the first one to touch it. Several days later, it was assembled and we spent a good hour one afternoon with me on the trainer (a trainer is a device that allows you to ride your bike indoors) and the owner of the bike shop making just minor adjustments until I was at the point that I felt comfortable on the bike.

On the first ride on my new bike, I was amazed at how much difference I could feel. It was definitely a faster bike. I just needed to settle down and get used to it. I had only three days before my second sprint. If my new bike felt good enough, I would give it a shot. That evening, I went out on a ride that was only seven miles and I didn't try to push it, I just wanted to gain some much-needed confidence in the bike before the race Saturday. Now if you have ridden a comfort bike with big tires you will appreciate what I am about to say. The differences between the old bike and new bike in weight, aerodynamics and position were unbelievable. I just started to pedal and looked down at my computer and I was doing 16 miles an hour and I was barely pedaling. Then I started down a small hill and stopped pedaling and the bike started to increase in speed and the next thing I knew, I was doing 23 miles down a hill not pedaling. On my old bike, I couldn't pedal that fast down the hill. Now not only did I have confidence in the way the bike felt, I had confidence in it being a faster bike.

Kestrel Talon

*Go for the moon. If you don't get it,
you'll still be heading for a star.
- Willis Reed -*

Nothing can stop the man with the right mental attitude from achieving his goal; nothing on earth can help the man with the wrong mental attitude.
- Thomas Jefferson -

- Chapter Eight -
My Second Triathlon

The second sprint would be a little longer. The distances were as follows: 400-yard swim – 15-mile bike – 2.5-mile run. I was confident that I could finish any of these distances, but just how well would I do? I tried to keep reminding myself that I should just have the goal of finishing, but I really wanted to do my best.

I had a much better idea of what to expect this time so my sleep the night before was much better. I jumped up the morning of the triathlon excited about the fact that it was my second sprint and I had a cool new bike. I had agreed to haul out a kayak so that the swim buoys could be put out on the swim course and someone could provide safety on the course for the swimmers. This would put me arriving earlier than usual to help get things going.

As I laid out my transition area, I couldn't help but notice that I was calmer than I had been on the first sprint. It all boiled down to the fact that I felt comfortable around the people who would be there. I also knew that many of my friends would be there and would accept me just the way I was. This time, I even took the time to talk to some of the other athletes and see what I could learn from them. The main thing was I was trying to stay calm and not worry about what was to come.

As we made our way to the swim, I remembered what my strategy was going to be: line up to the left of everyone and swim to the buoy on an angle. This would give the faster swimmers the chance to get out of the way and I could fall into my own pace and race my race. I even had a buddy who was going to line up next to me and since we were taking the same approach, I realized that I wasn't the only one having problems with the swim. When the race started, I stuck to my plan and was excited because I fell right into my relaxed stroke and proceeded on my slow, merry way. My swim did improve, but I had still not yet gained confidence in my stroke and kept checking my direction at least every 10 strokes. This was slowing me down even more because I was loosing my forward momentum - what little I had. I'm sure to the safety guy in the boat, I looked like a big barge or tugboat just crawling along, but still it was nice to hear some encouraging words like "You're looking good!" and "You're almost there!" And finally I *was* there. I came out of the water - not with a blazing time, but still I was fairly close to some of the other competitors, so that was an improvement.

In the transition area, I just took my time and tried not to rush or waste time and eventually I headed out on the bike. On the bike, I was making fairly good time, but was trying to hold back a little because I didn't want to be wasted on the run. Everything was going pretty well and then...

"THE PROBLEM FOR THE DAY." About a week before the race I had gone to the bike shop and had the owner readjust my bike seat with a minor adjustment. At the eight-mile mark, the nose of my bike seat just tilted downward and made for a very interesting ride. I had a choice to make: would I stop and try to repair it with the small tool kit that I carried on my bike or would I tough it out and ride on with my bike and my butt in this state? I decided to ride on in and be the tough guy, but that was not the smartest move that I had ever made. By not getting off and tightening up my bike seat, I had put myself in a position where I was riding with most of my weight on my hands and shoulders. As I made my way in mile by mile, this got more uncomfortable and before I knew it, it was just getting downright painful. After supporting most of my weight with my hands, arms and shoulders, I was whipped. I was literally shaking when I came into the transition area. I could barely get my shoes tied for the run because I was trembling so badly.

I managed to get my shoes halfway tied and I headed out on the run. As usual, I walked for the first part, trying to get my legs back from the bike leg. I had been doing intervals where I would run for two minutes and walk for two minutes, so I just converted that over to running from one electrical pole to the other and then I would walk to the next and so on. Eventually, I made it to the finish and could place my second sprint triathlon under my belt.

I would be remiss if I didn't give you this word of advice that I learned after this race: Something is not going to go your way in a race. It may be with your body or it may with equipment. Your biggest challenge will be not letting it determine if you don't finish. Be prepared - whether it's physically or mentally.

Don't Quit

When things go wrong as they sometimes will.
When the road you're trudging seems all up hill.
When funds are low and the debts are high.
And you want to smile, but you have to sigh.
When care is pressing you down a bit.
Rest, if you must, but don't you quit.
Life is queer with its twists and turns.
As every one of us sometimes learns.
And many a failure turns about
When he might have won had he stuck it out:

Don't give up though the pace seems slow -
You may succeed with another blow.
Success is failure turned inside out -
The silver tint of the clouds of doubt.
And you never can tell how close you are.
It may be near when it seems so far:
So stick to the fight when you're hardest hit
It's when things seem worst that you must not
QUIT.

Anonymous

*Go confidently in the
direction of your dreams.
Live the life you've imagined.
- Henry David Thoreau -*

- Chapter Nine -
My Third Sprint

One more sprint and the T-Shirt would be rightly mine...

A mere two weeks later was the last sprint of the training series. In those two weeks, I had gotten more comfortable with my bike and had improved my swim ever so slightly, but things were still improving.

During this time, one of our local Tri Club members in town heard me talking about how I just couldn't seem to get my run up and going and how I was discouraged by this fact. I was starting to get just far enough away from where I had started, that I was forgetting about how much improvement I had seen and still continued to see. He told me about a book that he had read and would let me borrow. It was titled **The Courage to Start: A Guide to Running for Your Life** by John "The Penguin" Bingham. This is a great book and I am thankful that he let me read it. You see, sometimes I tend to want to read books that are just about training and that is not always good. I have found that it is great if you are able to read books that are honest, realistic and inspirational. This book gave me a reality check and allowed me to get back in touch with my sense of what was motivating me to do this. It wasn't just for a great time - it was for my family, it was for me.

The big day came for the longest triathlon that I had done: 600-yd swim, 18-mile bike and a 3-mile run. I have to say that I was a little nervous because I had only had an additional week and a half to train for this event. This would push me to the limit and I thought I could handle it, but it would be a test to see if I had the tenacity to finish the race.

I used my same old strategy on the swim and started on the outside and let the faster swimmers go on out ahead of me. I then settled into my pace and set my eyes on the halfway mark and finally I was there. My buddy Brad was in the rescue kayak and offered me a few encouraging words as I made the turn. Finally, I made it to the shore and was excited that I was able to complete the swim. As I made it to the transition area, I focused on making an efficient transition to the bike.

My transition went fairly smoothly and I was able to get on the bike quickly. I kept trying to remind myself that it wasn't a race against anyone else but myself. I pedaled toward the halfway point and was averaging a decent speed for me, which excited me even more. I really didn't try to focus on anything but maintaining a constant speed and relaxing. As I made it to the halfway point and started back, I saw a biker in front of me and made it my goal to keep him in my sights. This might have been a mistake, but I pressed on and pedaled hard. Now you might remember that this is the same course with Mt. Everest coming in on the bike leg. As I rounded the corner for the last two and a half miles, there she was, Mt Everest. It was then that I came to the reality that I should have ridden my own race and not chased anyone down. As I proceeded up that hill, I had almost come to a halt. I had gotten so slow that I was able to read the gum wrappers and bottle caps on the ground. Why in the world did I think that I needed to chase that other rider? Well, what was done, was done and I had to keep on going. I made it up the hill and cruised to the bike finish.

I have to admit that I was surprised; I had had a good swim (which translates to no panic attack and I made it out alive), I had no mechanical problems on the bike, and so I should have a pretty good run. As I got off the bike and started out of the transition area, my calves and shins were burning, but it would go away, right? WRONG! After about a half mile, I was talking to myself about how, if I just did a mile that was okay. I could still be proud of doing even a mile. Upon arriving at the half-mile point, I decided to press on to where there was a mile turnaround point. Surely if I did a total of two miles, that would be respectable. As I plodded on, my feet were slapping the ground and I am sure that it probably sounded like I was running with scuba fins on. I was in severe pain, my calves and shins were burning like fire and I thought they might explode. At about that time, my buddy Brad came running by me and squirted me with cold water, and did it ever feel good! Brad, along with some of the other triathletes were training at longer distances than the official race lengths. At the time that was just kind of disgusting! I kept plodding on and there were friends passing me on the way in giving me words of encouragement. I made it to the one-mile turnaround and continued to press on. I was determined that I was going to do this. I remembered from the bike ride where the turnaround was for this race and I plodded on becoming more determined by the step. When I was about 100 yards from the turnaround, another one of my friends, John, started screaming that I was close and to just keep it up and I was going to make it.

As I made it to the turn around I noticed that my calves and shins were loosening up and I decided to run for about fifteen seconds to see how it felt. I was starting to push the edge of the envelope for myself physically and was pretty aware of it. As I moved along, I was able to run for a little longer each time. As I made each step, I knew that I was stepping toward accomplishing a bigger goal than I could have originally envisioned. By the time I was about a mile out, I was starting to see some of the faster racers coming toward me in cars. Oh, how embarrassing was this! They had probably already taken a shower and changed clothes and here I was, still fighting with myself on the run. As some of them started to pass, they would roll down the windows on their vehicles and give words of encouragement like, "Hang in there, Big Man!" "You're almost home!" "You're looking good!" "You can do it!" I have to admit that this is encouraging to you when you are almost physically spent and you just want to make it to the finish line. But then I didn't care if it was embarrassing or not. As John Bingham had said in his book, "it had taken *me* more courage to start, than it had taken *them* to finish."

Well, I did make it to the finish line and, yes, I did have some friends there waiting on me just as before. They were just as excited for me this time as they were when I completed my first.

That afternoon and the next day, I was whipped. I could tell I had pushed my body to a point that I couldn't remember pushing it to before. I told one of my friends who is a fairly accomplished triathlete that I was just drained. He told me that it even drained him. For me, it might as well been a Full Iron Man competition, I was tired and I would bet money that I was more physically drained than he was. With that being said, most people won't be able to relate to what you feel unless they have been there. If they haven't, just let them believe they understand. It will just make them feel better. One thing was certain...
I had earned the shirt.

Do not pray for easy lives.
Pray to be stronger men!
Do not pray for tasks
equal to your powers.
Pray for power equal to your tasks.
- Phillips Brooks -

It's not whether you get knocked down: it's whether you get up.
- Vince Lombardi -

- Chapter Ten -
Indian Creek 2002

f you remember, the first time I attended a triathlon was to work. Just like the first time, I was here to work again. My sound company was once again providing sound equipment and services for the triathlon.

The difference between the last sprint I had done and this one, was 200 yards extra on the swim, 2 extra miles on the bike and an extra tenth of a mile on the run. I was so close to being able to do it, and yet I felt so far away. I had told myself that it was okay that I wasn't going to be able to compete this year. After all, I had completed the last event in the training series and I should be satisfied with that.

As usual, my business partner and I had gone to the venue the evening before and started setting up for the event. We were confident that we could do a better job than last year and would have a good time doing it since we now knew what to expect. As we set up, I looked out across the transition area at all the volunteers setting up for the next day's event. They were smiling and laughing with each other. As the evening went on, I started to dream a little bit about what it would have been like to be a competitor in the event the next day. The rest of the evening was spent around the makeshift camp that we had set up so we could provide our own personal security for our equipment.

That night, I just couldn't sleep. I tossed and turned all night thinking about the next day's event. It was almost like I would actually be competing, but I knew that I wouldn't. I finally decided at 4:30 in the morning that I would get up and take a shower.

I walked back through the transition area just as volunteers started to arrive. As the sun started coming up over the transition area, the excitement started to build in my stomach. Then slowly, athletes started arriving and filling the transition area. It was at this time that the feeling of excitement started to turn into a sick feeling. I knew that I could do this triathlon. The distance was only slightly longer than the last one I had completed. Why had I avoided getting someone to work for me running sound so I could get out there and compete? It was too late to worry about it now, but I was just about ready to throw up.

Then and there, I made the decision that I would live with it and that the role I would take on would be one of the encourager. I knew that the words of encouragement that I had received had made a difference to me and I would do my best to pass that along. So that's what I did. I found somewhere in which I could encourage people to keep on going.

As I walked through the transition area, I spoke to different folks that I knew from our local tri club and others that I had gotten to know through other races. Then I ran across one of my friends. Now this particular individual is the one who had to be pulled from the water the year before because of problems on the swim and this year he was already suffering from anxiety in the transition area just thinking about the swim. Now I'm not trying to paint a picture of somebody standing there, being whiney. It's just when you are friends with someone, you know when they are worried about something. I took this as my first opportunity to try to encourage someone. I talked to him and told him that I had confidence in him and was sure that he would be able to do the swim if he just relaxed. I reminded him to let the other swimmers get ahead of him and that he should just settle down and get in his own pace. Talking to him might not of given him any inspiration or comfort, but hopefully it did. I tried to think about what I would feel like and what I would want to hear someone tell me. As I walked around the transition area, giving words of encouragement, I am sure that folks who didn't have any idea who I was probably thought I was just some crazy armchair triathlete - if that. Maybe in reality, I was just a wannabe, but I can tell you this much: it really didn't matter to me what they thought. If I could encourage one person, then that was what would make it worthwhile

I made my way over to the swim start area and mingled with the spectators before the start. We had set up a separate sound system for the start and I had positioned myself close by, but this put me in the middle of the spectators. There were people who had never seen a triathlon before and I could hear the normal buzz of questions, about how things would work, such as "Where is the start?" and "Where is the finish?" and "Are they really going to swim that far?" Of course, you always have the person in disbelief as to why anyone would want to do something like this. I heard the occasional "These have got to be the craziest people I have ever seen!" I certainly could relate because only a year before, I hadn't had a clue either.

If you have never been to a triathlon and been able to watch the start of the swim, you don't know what you're missing. You can sense the excitement and tension of the athletes as they anticipate that the starting time is drawing near. At the start, the water starts churning and swimmers jockey for position. Just watching the start doesn't even begin to give you an idea of what is really going on in the water. You don't get to see one competitor swimming over the top of another and feet kicking right in front of their faces and millions of tiny bubbles tickling your body as swimmers kick in front of you.

As the last wave left from the start area, I was able to break down the sound system and positioned myself at the exit of the swim to cheer on my friends and the folks that just wanted to finish. Because I was starting to become active in the sport of triathlon, I really started to listen to some of the spectators. It is great to hear a child asking their mom where their dad is or the silence of a husband as he eagerly awaits his wife's exit from the water. Something I noticed was some wives of the faster triathletes had stayed near the exit of the swim just so they could cheer on some of the last swimmers out of the water. There seem to be people like this at every triathlon willing to cheer on people that they don't know just because they appreciate the effort and dedication each of these athletes has made. I then moved to the bike transition area and started working in the dismount area. I had started assisting some of the other volunteers by warning the bikers that they were about to approach the dismount area and they needed to slow down.

You see this was another defining moment in this year of training. I had made the choice to use this as a learning experience and be an encourager. So I started cheering people on and watching their faces. You could see some with just pure agony on their faces, but they kept plodding on. You could see some faces that were all smiles as they were just enjoying the experience. I did see one mother with fear on her face because she had apparently missed her son as he made his way out of the water and didn't know if he had made it in on the bike. As I mingled with the crowd, I saw that there was just one relay team left and the runner for the relay team was just pacing back and forth. The team feared that the biker had either wrecked on the bike course or he could have had mechanical problems with his bike. Then I learned the biker they were waiting on was a young man in his early teens. As he entered the dismount area, there was a relief on the faces of his family and friends. This should remind us all that as safe as we try to make the sport, the waiting can be the hardest for our family and friends.

One by one, people crossed the finish line from the run and just as always in triathlons, the more time that accumulated on the clock, the smiles got bigger and bigger on the competitors.

The awards ceremony was great and a couple of friends who had not seen me in several months came up to me and asked what I was doing because they could tell that I had lost weight. I began telling them about the journey that I had been on thus far and how I was training to try to be thinner, better and faster. You start building a relationship with folks who appreciate what you can do as an overweight athlete. Most of them realize the physical stamina that it takes them to finish a race and know that you have to reach deep down within yourself to find whatever it takes to move you to the finish line.

The day was rapidly ending and I could chalk it up as another learning experience. I didn't compete, but I learned as much - or more than I would have if I competed.

"But they that wait upon the Lord shall renew their strength; They shall mount up with wings as eagles; They shall run, and not be weary; and They shall walk, and not faint."
       - Isaiah 40:31 -
       - Holy Bible -

Far better it is to dare mighty things, to win glorious triumphs, even though checkered by failure, than to take rank with those poor spirits who neither enjoy much nor suffer much, because they live in the gray twilight that knows not victory nor defeat."
- Theodore Roosevelt -

- Chapter Eleven -
Bare Bones Tri

ust being a spectator was enough to make me want to keep on training. I had a longing to do a big triathlon and I was going to do it that same year. I had learned of a "Bare Bones" series that was put on around the Lake Charles area. I looked into going to the second race in that series which was in June. I tried to find a couple of buddies to go with me, but there was another race that weekend and I had to make the decision to go by myself to face the unknown alone. I had grown very comfortable around my friends at the three sprint training events and knew that they had accepted me, but if I went out of town, what would these people think about me showing up to their event? I called and spoke to the race director for this event and was assured that the bike course and run were flat and the distances were what I could handle, so I said, "Sign me up!"

I had about a month to train and in the mean time, I had decided to do my first major event, which was the Sports Spectrum River Cites Triathlon to be held in August. The Bare Bones event would be a good training event en route to my first major event. Well, for some unknown reason, I decided that in a two-month time period, I needed to try to lose 30 pounds so I could go into the race in August just that much lighter.

I started a low-carb diet, which was a complete change from the healthy meals that I had been eating. I didn't change my way of training and was still training hard but was suffering from a lack of energy. After about two weeks, I started having severe stomach pains two hours after I ate and they continued to worsen. I am not a big fan of going to the doctor, but I was at the point that the pain was getting intolerable. Although nothing was determined at the time, the doctor decided later that that he thought it had been a combination of a virus that was going around, acid reflux, and the sudden change in my diet. I went into the Bare Bones sprint having consumed nothing for the five previous days except Gatorade and soup with some crackers. To top this off, I had suffered from diarrhea for over two weeks and was fairly weak, but decided to press on. You see, I have already told you that something seems to go wrong for each race and that was what this was.

The day before the race, I drove to Lake Charles and spent the night so I wouldn't have to get up and drive in early on race morning. My wife didn't go with me since she knew our son would likely keep me up all night and she knew I needed some peace and quiet before the event. I still had trouble sleeping the night before and raced the race over in my head a hundred times until it was time to get up. When I arrived at the race site, there were a few people already there and getting ready for the race. Now, remember when you're an oversized athlete, you are going to get some looks from the little guys because they realize that this won't be a cakewalk for them and they wonder how you are going to do this if they are going to struggle with it.

This is where we must learn our next lesson: it doesn't matter what someone looks like, how old or how young they are, they may just be better than you and, yes, they could be worse than you. It goes back to don't judge a book by its cover.

In a Bare Bones, Tri it for Fun, Tri it Naked, short race series or training series, you will notice that the event is put on for the purpose of training and to let the first-timers come out and try it on a less intimidating course. You will also probably notice that many of the little guys who are first timers will come up and ask you questions about your readiness, which will give them a vote of confidence if you say you're ready.

On the morning of this sprint, as I unloaded my bike, a gentleman pulled up beside me and got out of the truck with a smile on his face and said good morning. The parking area for the event ran parallel to about half of the swim and I noticed that he was looking very warily at the swim course.

As I looked up from my bike, he said, "That sure looks like a long way to have to swim."

I had, by this time, done enough sprints to know that for some reason it always looks kind of long no matter what the distance and I reassured him "Don't worry. Just remember that if you don't make it out of the water you can't finish."

We made our way to the transition area, signed in and started getting prepared for the race. Let me throw this little bit of information in for you and remember it will be important a little later on. It was a big step for me to ride my bike in bike shorts and now I had started racing in tri shorts because they are just better for running. Tri shorts are much like bike shorts except they are cut to provide comfort for running, whereas bike shorts are specifically designed to give you support when you are riding a bike. If you are a spectator at a triathlon you will notice a lot of racers swim in tri shorts, ...not me. I put on a pair of swim trunks on over my tri shorts and pull them off after the swim. Somewhere in the United States, I am sure that there is a Clydesdale doing the same thing, however, I have no documentation of this. Even if there isn't, I do because it makes me feel more comfortable.

I have to say that Mark and Diane Tarver of Tri Specialties in Sulphur, Louisiana, did a great job putting on their Bare Bones Series. They limited it to 100 racers and before you start, you know what's going on and what the rules are. If you are within driving distance of Sulphur, you would enjoy giving an introductory race like this one a shot for your first race. (Just before this book was published Mark and Diane Tarver made the decision not to have the Bare Bones Series, but if you are interested in a short race such as this, just look around and you can find one that is also a great race.)

Let's get to the race. I will start with the swim. If you are a first-time triathlete or feel that you are a slow swimmer, the Tarver's allowed athletes to choose to start in the 3rd wave. I chose the third wave just because I knew that I was not a fast swimmer. This swim started and ended at a boat dock and athletes walked down a boat ramp to get in the water and up a boat ramp to exit. My first clue that the ramp was a little slimy should have been the race workers laying a runner of indoor carpet down the boat ramp, but I didn't put two and two together.

As my wave made its way down the ramp and into the water, I noticed that people were proceeding without moving their feet and that was really odd. As I reached the water and started down the ramp, I felt a nice layer of slime under my feet and as I got about waist deep, I felt myself losing my balance and my feet going forward. At that instant, I knew that I really needed to look cool so I just tried to make it look as though I had planned the whole thing and slipped gracefully into the water until my head disappeared below the surface of the water. Well, it felt graceful. For all I know, I could have looked like a struggling manatee in the Florida Keys. As I looked over to my right, I quickly forgot about my graceful move when I saw one of the triathletes hanging onto the pier before the start.

My wave started and I got right into my stroke. It seemed that I had been swimming no time when I passed a buoy on my left. My first thought was that I had made it to the first buoy so I tried to get my bearings on the second buoy. I couldn't find the second buoy. Then I looked around and realized that I was *at* the second buoy! I was thinking, "Great! I am having a decent swim." I made the turn and I encountered my first problem for the day, the sun was in my eyes and I was swimming with a pair of clear goggles that were starting to fog up. This made the swim back in a little more interesting for me. I couldn't tell where I was going and ended up getting off course, which did hurt my time a little, but I somehow made it in. I'll tell you why I really made it in: there was a nice young lady lifeguard that was one of the lifeguards for the event. She was carrying a big red rescue buoy that was about four feet long. If you have never seen one, it is like an over grown pool noodle. As I began to get off course, she was so thoughtful, and started slap her rescue buoy on the water and scream in a kind voice "Sir, ...Sir... you are off the course!" Well, hopefully this was my problem for the day.

I made a fairly good transition to the bike leg and was on my way, when I encountered my second problem. I couldn't get my bike to shift onto the big sprocket. I ended up spinning at a higher cadence than I had intended for about 8 miles, but at mile eight, I hit a bump and tried to shift my bike and the chain went to the big sprocket. Because of this, I was able to pass a few people on the bike.

My run was, as usual, horrible. I just couldn't get to the point where I could keep going for a long distance. Even in training, when I was fresh, my legs would just give out at about an eighth of a mile. Everybody that I had passed on the bike passed me on the run and that just made me feel like crap. But I finished and that was the good thing. After the race, an elderly gentlemen came up to me and told me just to hang in there and that I had a decent swim and that I had a really good bike. I thought that my bike was just mediocre and the swim was alright, but he took the time to come by and give me a word of encouragement.

About three weeks later was the last race in this series and I decided to do it because it would give me another good training race before my biggest race in August. You know, you just have to laugh sometimes at things that happen to you and this race would have a few things that would be memorable.

I arrived race morning and proceeded to lay out my transition area, and as I looked up, this guy said, "Well Michael Pate, are you ready for the swim?"

I responded, "Yes, I think so," but with a look of *who are you?*

I finally walked over to his bike and said, "I'm sorry, but I don't guess I know who you are."

He responded, "I'm the guy who beat you out of the water by ten seconds the last race."

This guy didn't mean anything by it, but he really didn't have to bring that up.

The night before the race, I had debated on whether I would make my debut swim in my tri shorts. And finally I had decided that I would swim in just the tri shorts and it was going to be okay. I had even gone so far as leaving my swimming trunks at the hotel room so that I wouldn't bail out on myself. That morning as I walked to the swim area, I saw...No, please God, tell me that isn't a news crew with a camera at the start! Why, yes, it was and I had to wonder how they had found out that this was my debut in my tri shorts on the swim? Maybe I would blend in with the other racers. Yeah, a 322-pound guy will blend into this crowd.

Well, at least I wasn't from the area and didn't have any friends in the local area who would be looking for me.

I had a good swim, which translates to not coming out of the water last, and that was my goal on the swim. I was a little bit more comfortable on the bike course, but on the way back in last time, I had timed my race perfectly for the dismissal of a small church and this time was no different. About a half a mile ahead of me, I could see people leaving the church and getting into their vehicles. Because I had been riding for a few months, I was well aware that people just don't look for people on bicycles. As I got even with the front of this church, an S.U.V. pulled right out in front of me and I had to brake hard to keep from hitting the rear quarter panel. In fact, after the vehicle pulled out, the driver wanted to cruise along at five miles an hour and finally decided to speed up. I ended up passing several people on the bike and went into the run with a little bit of a lead over the other competitors. This is where I learned one of the most valuable lessons of the entire year of training. ***Don't give up. Don't leave any race knowing you could have raced a little harder.*** As I was out on the run, several people passed me and then two more people passed me and I was positive that this put me in last place, and that just took the wind out of my sails. I gave up and resorted to just finishing. As I made the turn around point, I could see two people running toward me. Maybe I was wrong, I needed to kick it up a notch and I could finish without being last. I started running. As I got near these two runners, I thought I recognized them as being some faster triathletes, and they may very well have been, but I assumed that they were just doing a cool-down run and why should I bust my butt to try to outrun someone on a cool-down run? If I just maintained my pace, I would beat my time from 3 weeks before and that should be enough. Well, those two folks ran me down and as they passed me and got about 100 yards ahead of me, I noticed they were looking back at me. But what the heck, they were just

92

cooling down. Two days after the race when results were posted, I learned that I had finished two minutes behind these two competitors. Now, I don't know if I had of kept running if they would have chased me down, but because I didn't give it my all, I will always wonder.

Let others lead small lives,
but not you.
Let others argue over small things,
but not you.
Let others cry over small hurts,
but not you.
Let others leave their future
in someone else's hands,
but not you.

- Jim Rohn -

"Success is not measured by what you accomplish but by the opposition you have encountered, and the courage with which you have maintained the struggle against overwhelming odds."
- Orison Swett Marden -

- Chapter Twelve -
River Cities Triathlon

fter the last race, I had roughly three weeks to prepare for River Cities Triathlon. I had a breakthrough on my running or slogging or whatever you call it, and now had actually made it 3.2 miles without stopping. The running had all seemed to be a mental challenge because I made it to a mile and a half then two, then two and a half and before I knew it I had done 3.2 miles without stopping. I will be the first to tell you that it was not a fast pace but it was faster than walking and I was building a base. My biking had seemed to improve and people were giving me compliments on how they were impressed with my ability as a big guy. A week out from the race, I was starting to get a case of the nerves from just not knowing what to expect. This race would have around 1000 competitors; I had entered into the Clydesdale division and was assured that there would be some elite Clydesdales there.

I ate properly the week before to try to build up a little energy reserve and tapered my workout schedule according to what had worked for me in my limited past experience. I increased my intake of water to try to prepare for the excessive heat that I would encounter on race day, but in the back of my mind was the question: *Was my preparation for this race going to be adequate?* I finally reached a point where I relented to the fact that I would be at least a finisher and I would give it my best to have a personal record, based on my splits from the shorter distance races. I had decided that based on my past races that if I finished in three hours, I should be happy.

Finally the day before the race arrived. I had made arrangements to travel to the race the day before, complete my packet pick-up and spend the night before the race within twenty minutes of the race site. This particular race is known for having an outstanding race packet. My race packet included three shirts, a tank top, a pair of socks, a pair of running shorts, a water bottle, some energy bars, a cap and a nice back pack. Even if you didn't have a good race you felt like a winner already.

After picking up my race packet, I went and checked into my hotel room and called my friend Jay. Jay was going to take me to the race site so that I could acclimate myself to it somewhat and would not feel so lost the next morning. We walked through the bike transition area and I found the location of my bike rack and then we proceeded to the swim. I looked out over the swim and there were buoys already in place. My first comment to Jay was that they must have spread the buoys out so they could work in the area, because the swim would be long if they didn't. The race area was fairly nice and Jay assured me that the bike had some hills with about 5 percent grades on them, but it's a fairly easy ride. The run course would offer some shade and would be mostly flat with a few hills and one portion that was a trail run. So off I went back to the hotel for dinner and to double-check my transition layout for the next day.

After eating a sandwich for dinner, I sat down and started reading over my race packet to make sure I had everything for race check-in. As I read through the packet, I saw the usual notes about drafting and being on time etc., but then there was something that just stuck out like a sore thumb. This race had cut-off times and that would be as follows swim: 9:00; bike: 10:30; run: 11:30. Now this was a shock to me because in my mind, I could make the bike and run cut-off but the swim cut-off? That was bothering me. I was starting in the last wave and if I got off course or had any problems I could end up on the bubble and get yanked off the course. This would give me 32 minutes after my wave started to make the swim and be out of the water if it was an actual half-mile.

I have to be real honest; I started to doubt my ability to get out of the water before the cut-off time. I had within the last few weeks made a swim in the pool of 800 yards at around 24 minutes but my past experience had indicated that I tended to have a slower time in open water and it would put me at about 28 minutes with no problems. I was almost sick thinking about how much and how hard I had trained in order to be able to at least finish this race and to even have the remote possibility of being pulled out of the race was almost sickening. I read about the cut off times again, thinking that it would depend on start time and we would have as much time to finish as the first wave, but that just wasn't how it read. I would have been better off competing in my age group than in the Clydesdale division and would simply have more time that way, but it was too late now to worry about that.

I called my wife and she could hear the panic in my voice concerning the cut-off time. I tried to sound calm about it, but we have been married long enough that she can sense when something is bothering me. She assured me that I could do it. She reminded me that I had worked so hard and had come so far and that I could achieve this goal. I also knew that as soon as we said goodbye, she started praying for me. I got into bed at 8:00 and was doing my best to clear my head of any negative thoughts but just tossed and turned for most of the night.

I woke up at 4:30 am on race morning and started my morning by drinking a bottle of water and taking a shower. I had butterflies and the swim cut-off time dominated my thoughts. I had a banana and an energy bar for breakfast and began to load my vehicle before heading out to the race. By 5:20 A.M., I was packed up and ready to check out of the hotel room. My plan was to arrive just before the gate opened so that I could park nearer to the transition area. I arrived at the gate to the race at 5:50 A.M. and there was already a line of cars waiting to get into the gate. I decided to get out of my vehicle and go ahead and get things ready on my bike such as putting on my computer and getting my water bottles on the bike. While I was doing this, several of the folks waiting in line with me began to talk about bikes and where they were from. Folks had driven in from Florida, Arkansas, Texas, and Oklahoma and from all parts of Louisiana.

A little after 6:00 A.M., the gate opened and we proceeded to the first parking area. Within two minutes, it was full and the masses started unloading their bikes and heading to the transition area to rack their bikes and lay out their transition areas. As I checked in my equipment, and moved my bike to my designated bike rack, I noticed that the buoys for the swim were still where they were from the day before and apparently were the markers for the swim course, which seemed awfully long. But then and there, I decided that I just had to focus on swimming my race and coming out of the water as fast as I could.

Later, I read this quote from **lafayettefitness.org**:

The "800 meter" swim was long. Probably 950 or more. I heard numbers from one and a half to three minutes as people noted how much slower they were than usual for a half mile.

Reading that quote reassured me that I had been right in thinking that the course looked unusually long.

The transition area was becoming fuller by the second. I made my way to the tattooing station to get my race markings. The walk from the parking area to the transition area had gotten me warmed up and I was sweating profusely, partially due to the heat and partially due to the fact that I was nervous. The poor lady trying to mark me with the Sharpie Marker was having a grand old time trying to write on my perspiring body, she even made the comment that "It's a little early to be sweating, isn't it?" I just told her that real Clydesdales came to the race already warmed up and ready to go.

I saw several people that I knew and we talked about what we had been doing the last couple of months and just exchanged pleasantries. You know by now that I have a philosophy that something is probably going to happen unexpectedly on race day, and I have a couple of examples for you. I spoke to one of the ladies from the tri club and she had gotten everybody loaded up and ready to leave from the hotel, but had forgotten to bring her own front wheel to her bike. Do you think she was suffering from a little anxiety? Oh, yeah! One of the other tri club members got to the race and he had a flat on his bike, and began changing his tube. As he started to air it up, there was a loud pop - he had busted another tube. He spent the next 30 minutes trying to find a tube from another competitor. He did find one, but by the time he had gotten it changed, he walked up right before his wave was going to start. So remember that almost anything can happen. You just need to figure out a way to overcome whatever it is.

Time passed and before long, everyone was making their way to the swim and they were getting close to starting the first wave. Now sometimes you will go to an event and you just realize that the event has been thoroughly planned out and some things are just overkill.

About five minutes before the start of the race, there was a loud explosion and I felt the sound waves hit my chest. I knew that I was already nervous, but when this happened, it took me about five seconds to float back down to the ground. The race director had employed someone with a cannon to fire it at the start of each wave so that you had no doubt when you would go. This thing was so loud that you could honestly see the sound waves shake the water, and I guess since we were in the heart of Dixie, there was nothing like a good ole fashion cannon to get things started.

Finally the start of the final wave was near and we all made our way out into the water. With an earth-shaking BOOM, we were off and on our way. I had been the person who had been kicked and hit in other triathlons, but not this time, I knew what to expect and I was dishing it out. I swam over a few people and kicked a few before the pack spread out and everyone was in their own little zone. I pulled along until I made it to the first buoy and then I made it to the second and turned on the backside of the swim. Now the comforting factor about the swim is that there are kayaks and canoes with lifeguards in them along the way and usually some powerboats that are for quick rescue. As I made the turn on the back side of the swim I encountered the strong taste of outboard motor oil in the water. Before you ask, no, I haven't ever tasted any before. It just tastes like it smells, and it started to kind of make me queasy. I was determined that this wasn't going to stop me so on I went. At about 100 yards out, I started to gag, but I just kept dog paddling hoping I wouldn't throw up in the water, and I would put my feet down just to see if I could touch the bottom. As soon as my feet could touch the bottom, I started walking and then started to run out of the water, because I didn't know what my time would be. As I hit the beach, my stopwatch was showing around 30 minutes and I just needed to get across the timing sensors fairly quickly in order to beat the cut-off for the swim. Now I didn't hear of anyone not making the cut-off time and maybe it wasn't enforced, but even if it had been, I was out of the water in time and on my way before the cut-off.

My transition to the bike leg was not the fastest in the world. I was patient and made my way out onto the bike course. My friends had told me that the bike course was fairly flat, with some rolling hills. First, I needed to consider the source and that being accomplished triathletes who weigh less than 200 lbs. Their definition of fairly flat with some rolling hills is different from mine. It seemed all uphill and was only flat long enough to let me start dreading the next hill. Anyway, as I have grown accustomed, I started to reel some folks in on the bike and before the four-mile mark I had reeled in two folks and had my eye on a group of riders ahead of me. As I had just passed my second bike, I started up a fairly long incline and started spinning as I went up the hill. I was doing my best to not let my cadence or my r.p.m.'s drop down to low on the bike and this is when I encountered a problem. As I shifted, my chained jumped off one sprocket and passed the next and the chain came off. It not only came off, it wrapped around the derailleur and the back sprocket and the front sprocket and looked like the backlash on a fishing reel. As I sat on the side of the road, the two bikers I had passed then passed me and I was back where I had started. Finally after about five minutes, I had it back on the sprockets and off I went. Eventually I reeled in the two other bikers and a few others and came in off the bike course with about a 1:13 time, which I was pretty satisfied with since I had lost about five minutes working on my bike.

My transition from the bike to the run went pretty smoothly and some of the tri club members were rooting me on. I went out on the run and was determined to give it my all. I still had visions of giving up on the run a few weeks earlier and that just wasn't going to happen this time. In my mind, I knew that I just couldn't leave anything on the run course. I had to walk a little, but as soon as I could, I started running and repeated the process when necessary. I kept waiting for the sound of a runner to come up behind me and overtake me, but by the halfway mark, nobody had passed me. As I made the two-mile mark, I could see some competitors coming down the run, but I just kept telling myself that if they caught me, they were going to have to earn it. I picked up my pace, focused on the road ahead of me and kept going. I saw a couple of runners in front of me and I started trying to chase them down. I could see that they were walking and running, but they were walking more than me and I had less than a mile to catch them. As I started getting close to the ½ mile to go mark, there were increasing numbers of people that were starting to give me words of encouragement. At the ¼ mile left to go mark, there were people all along the sides of the run who were yelling at me to finish strong. At the 1/8th left to go mark, I turned it up and gave it all I had. I could hear people toward the finish line cheering me on, but at about 100 yards out from the finish line, the cheers went away, the announcers voice faded away and it was just me and the finish line. I was going to finish and I was going to beat my projected time by at least fifteen minutes, if not more. As I crossed the finish line, I was given my finisher's medal which might as well been a gold medal.

Okay, let's stop right here with the whole *Chariots of Fire* music and get into what I will *really* be remembered for. Have you heard about dehydration? Well, let me tell you about it. It's not a good idea to drink water on the swim leg for obvious reasons. People forget however, that you are sweating in the water, so it is important that you drink fluids on the bike to stay hydrated. You remember when I told you about the chain coming off my bike? Well, after I got back on the bike, I didn't focus on drinking fluids. I focused on chasing down other riders and didn't drink much on the bike. So when I got to the run, even though I was drinking fluids, I was a little late on replenishing them. To top it off, I had tried to run like a madman to the finish line, which further unnecessarily drained my body of fluids. After crossing the finish line, I was weak, very weak, and asked my buddy Jay to get me something to drink while I sat down under a tree to try to get my strength back. He brought me back something that said Gatorade concentrate but I couldn't tell much difference between it and lake water. After I had sat on the ground for a while, Jay told me that I needed to get up and walk it off. Being the mountain of a man that I am, I lumbered to my feet. That's when things started turning yellow. I remember talking to a friend, then feeling my knees hit the ground and then I was lying down. On the way down, I remember thinking that I was going to be really dirty when I got up, but after I hit, it sure did feel good to lie down.

As would fate would have it, I was only twenty-five feet from the ambulance and the paramedics when I hit the deck. It had been a slow day for them, with no bike wrecks and only having to give one other I.V. You may be asking me how I know this, well they hooked me up to every medical gadget they had on that ambulance. I swear that you don't get checked over that well when you go to the doctor! I was hooked up to so much stuff that I was picking up HBO and Cinemax. Finally they insisted that I ride on the stretcher to the medical tent, which was a whopping fifteen feet away. Of course, I told them that I could walk, but they insisted that I take a little ride, so I did. They must have thought that it was a NASCAR race because the strapped me in so well I could hardly move. After they got me over to the tent they unhooked some of the stuff because I couldn't even get local t.v. channels and then they started an I.V. Then they started running a blood sugar test on me and I was getting worried as to what they would do next, so out of nervousness, I started to joke around with the paramedics.

After about a half of a bag of fluid, I was feeling good and that's when an old man walked over to me and said "You don't need to be doing these thangs till you loose some weight." You have heard that some people need to wear a sign around their neck that says "I'm Stupid"? All I can say is that he must have forgotten where he left his sign.

In the heat of the moment, I told him, "Buddy, you need to go get on your little old people scooter and ride off into the sunset." I think at that moment, the paramedics were really happy that they had me strapped in because I was about ready to kick me some senior citizen booty. Now don't start trying to track me down because you think that I dislike those who are my elders. He was just a rude sarcastic old toot and I wasn't in the mood to turn the other cheek. Anyway, after two bags of I.V. fluid, I was released from the medical tent and was told I was okay.

The days to come would prove that hitting the deck would be hard to live down.

99.9% is NOT Good Enough!

IF 99.9% IS GOOD ENOUGH, THEN...

- *Two million documents will be lost by the I.R.S. this Year*

- *Twenty two thousand checks will be deducted from the wrong bank accounts in the next hour*

- *Two Babies will be given to the wrong parents each day*

- *Thirteen thousand three hundred fourteen phone calls will be misplaced by telecommunications services every minute*

- *Two plane landings daily at O'Hare will be unsafe*

- *291 pacemaker operations will be performed incorrectly this year*

- *107 incorrect medical procedures will be performed today*

- *18,322 pieces of mail will be mishandled in the next hour.*

"No one knows what he can do until he tries."

- Publilius Syrus -

- Chapter Thirteen -
Okay, I Came, I Saw,
I Passed Out...Now What?

For the next several weeks, everyone was asking if I had passed out lately. Some people will take every opportunity to give you a little ribbing. I have to admit that I like to pick on people about things and all the times that I had picked on other folks would make my turn draw out for a while. Well, I had success in my training because I had been training for specific events and after Sports Spectrum I had set my sites on racing in a 5K in October. I stepped up my training in the run and it was getting better. I reached the point where I was running/jogging/slogging or whatever you want to call it for an hour. I had also helped to get a group of riders together for a Saturday morning ride and this helped me have some accountability for riding the bike.

On a humid Saturday morning in late August, I met for the first ride of our newly-formed riding group. We had a great group for the first day and we had decided that we would only make about a fifteen-mile ride since we had some folks showing up to ride for the first time. As we left from the parking lot where we had gathered, we approached a traffic light. I was ahead of the group by about twenty five yards and decided that instead of waiting, I would proceed through the green light and wait for the group on the other side. As I pedaled across the intersection, I had one of the biggest surprises I had ever had on a bike. My front wheel dropped off into an expansion joint. If you don't know what an expansion joint is, I'll be more than happy to explain. When streets are poured from concrete, pieces of wood are placed every so many feet, usually about twenty feet, to allow the pavement to expand and constrict with the temperature extremes. Now this is not an excerpt from the magazine *Engineering Weekly*, but hopefully you get the picture. Since I was crossing a major intersection, I was going the same direction as the expansion joints. The events that unfolded as I hit that expansion joint seemed like one of those action movies slow motion scenes. My tire and wheel dropped down about 2 inches and wedged which momentarily caused my bike to come to a sudden halt. When it stopped, I didn't. I proceeded over the handlebars, and since my bike was attached to my feet, it started coming behind me. Somewhere, while in the air, I came unclipped from my bike and it flew off in another direction while I hurtled toward the ground. Because it is just a natural instinct to stick out your arm to break your fall, I did and started to break my fall when my hand and wrist hit the pavement. Next my forearm and elbow hit and my elbow took most of the blow. I then hit with my hip and knee and rolled and ended up standing on my feet. I knew that I had hit pretty hard but everything seemed to be working except that the area around my elbow hurt a little. I grabbed my bike and checked it out and it looked okay, except for the chain being off. I put the chain back on, assured everybody that I was fine and started my ride. As the ride progressed, my right arm started to get stiff, but, hey, I just had a pretty good fall and that was to be expected. I completed the ride and had to rush home to get ready for a brunch in town that my sound company was providing equipment for. I called my wife from the parking lot to tell her about my wreck and she was immediately concerned. I told her I was fine and that I had even completed the ride. After arriving home and getting in the shower, I noticed that my arm was really starting to swell and I was really starting to have a limited range of motion. I still brushed off the whole deal and decided that I was just supposed to be sore and the swelling was just part of the whole deal. When I showed my wife that I couldn't straighten my arm, she began to insist that I go to the emergency room, but I told her that I didn't have time since I had a prior commitment.

I attended the brunch and noticed that I was losing almost all mobility in my arm. I couldn't even move it away from my body. The swelling continued and I had almost unbearable pain when I moved my arm. When I arrived home, I started putting ice packs on it and it seemed to be better, but it still hurt like the devil. I just didn't want to go to the emergency room and sit there for hours.

That same afternoon, I realized that I was apparently getting worse by the hour. I called one of my friends who is my personal physician and told him that I didn't want to go to the ER and asked him what I could do, He told me that he was on call and that he thought I should just run by his house and see him when he got home. After explaining to him how the accident occurred and what I was feeling, he said that it probably wasn't broken, but if the swelling didn't go down by Monday morning I needed to come by his office and have my arm x-rayed.

Sunday was absolutely miserable. I couldn't move without gasping in pain and by Monday morning, I had gotten to the point that I knew that I was going to the doctor's office first thing. X-rays were taken and later that morning I received a call from my doctor who said, "Michael, you fractured your arm at the joint!" When I asked what our treatment plan would be he said, "I don't know what we need to do, so let's send you to an orthopedist." Well, my arm was still extremely swollen and more x-rays were taken at the orthopedic office. The orthopedist said that the swelling was bad enough that it was difficult to tell how bad things were and that he thought at the very least it was a non-displaced fracture.

Now meeting with the orthopedist was kind of funny when I look back at it. Just picture in your mind me walking into the office. I am not a little guy, six one and 316 pounds so you can imagine when I tell him how this happened what he is going to think. First, I had to meet with the nurse who asked me how I hurt myself and I explained the story to him and he took me back to x-ray. After x-rays, I was moved to a room and was waiting for the doctor when the nurse came in and asked me to tell him again how the accident had happened and then he left. Then the doctor walked in and saw me for the first time and said, "So you had a little bike accident?" and I acknowledged that was correct, but we had not communicated effectively, because he thought that I was talking about a motorcycle.

The rest of the visit was to tell me that for the next three weeks, I couldn't run, bike or swim. I have to say that I left that appointment absolutely crushed. For the last year, my life had been consumed with God, Family, Work and Training and now he had told me I had to quit training cold turkey for three weeks. I was actually scared to death that the routine that had become second nature was going to somehow leave or pass me by just like people had passed and left me on the run.

The next few weeks were miserable. I just couldn't sit on the stationary bike for any length of time and I felt like my whole life had been disrupted. I overheard my wife telling someone that I was not a pleasant person to live with and I admit, I was out of my mind, worrying about what this would do to me.

Finally the orthopedist released me to go back to riding and to running. Biking seemed to improve after the time off, while on the other hand running had taken a turn for the worst. I had increased my run time by about seven minutes and my lungs burned when I ran. Psychologically this was an obstacle that I had been dreading and hoped that it wouldn't affect me at all, but soon I realized that it was a battle that I just couldn't avoid. Over the next few weeks, I just had problems making time for a run. Before the accident, I had been able to go for a run regardless of my schedule and if it meant getting up early or running at night I had been ready and willing to make the sacrifice to do this.

Over the next few weeks, I decided that I would try to continue to train for the 5K but wasn't totally committed to the event. Finally, I decided that I was going to do it and even if I hadn't trained, it would be a good psychological test for me and I could work on my mental toughness. Over the next four weeks, I only managed about one run a week and those were absolutely to me tougher than any of the triathlons that I had been in.

My motto was always to keep swinging. Whether I was in a slump or feeling badly or having trouble off the field, the only thing to do was keep swinging.
- Hank Aaron -

Step up the stairs or stare at the steps.
- Ralph Nichols -

- Chapter Fourteen -
Let's Do A 5K

For months, I had noticed that I had, without intending to, given some inspiration to other people. What was mind-boggling to me was the people who would come up to me and say that they just didn't understand or believe that I could do what I was doing in triathlons. They said that if I was able to do what I was doing, then it inspired them to try to reach down and find something that they didn't know they had in them. I never had the intention of having that affect on anyone. I knew that some people decided they would try the sport of triathlon because if a big guy like me could do it, then they thought they could. Now you may think that would offend me, but it didn't. Going against what was viewed as the norm and showing people not to judge a book by its cover was neat. If every time I raced it motivated someone to start training then that was good enough for me.

Finally the day came for my first official 5K. I had done the distance in a triathlon, which I had walked probably a third of the way. I had completed four miles without stopping, but that was before my bike wreck. I knew going in I had not trained enough, but I had always heard that it was better to be under-trained than over-trained. I think that guys who haven't trained say that to make themselves feel a little better. My goal was just to make the whole distance without stopping to walk. I wanted to run my race, and even if it meant I slowed to a jog that was slower than I could walk, I was going to hang in there and prove to myself that I could do it.

My whole goal was to start out not watching pace, but watching my heartrate monitor. I would bump up to 160 and I would hold that until the last mile. Then I would bump up to 170 and save a little for a kick. I felt that I could do this and make about a 13:30 first mile and then would make the second at about the same pace then would hopefully have a faster last mile. I had never gone out on the course but was somewhat familiar with the area and didn't foresee any surprises.

The day before the race, I made my way to the registration/packet pickup and picked up my race packet. I had the occasion to talk to some of my fellow tri club members and pass the pleasantries and learn about some of the events they had recently competed in. I really didn't pay any attention to my race packet, specifically my bib number until I got home. As I looked at my bib number, I saw that they had me racing as one year younger than I actually was and they also had me as a female. I had never raced as a female and I was absolutely positive that I was male, so I got in touch with registration and we got that straightened out.

Local weather had predicted a race temperature of about 63 degrees - which would be Clydesdale-friendly - and sunshine. Race day weather was a sunny 72 degrees with 100 percent humidity, just the kind of weather I love to race in! The air was as thick as syrup and you needed gills to breathe in it. I was running around the pre-race event talking to different people and letting them know about my sound company and talking to old friends and making new ones, when suddenly it was time to start. My wife and son wished me well and I headed up to the start area. I had a couple of people that I was going to start with but they were buried in the crowd and had made their way up into the middle of the pack. I knew that we were in the wrong place, but I had decided I would stick with them. The gun fired and we were off. For some odd reason, this start seemed like the start of the first swim I had made in my first triathlon. I felt like I had never run before and that I was smothering. I made my way to the outside of the pack trying to find a place where I could settle into my pace, but it just wasn't happening. At the first quarter mile mark, my heartrate was at 170 and I knew that this wasn't my race plan. The guys I was running with were, in my opinion, taking it out too fast but it was their race to run as they pleased.

I made the decision that I would slow down and try to get my heartrate down to 160 and then run the race that I had anticipated running. As I got within 100 yards of the 1st mile marker, I saw one of my friends and he was yelling for me to slow down. I *had* slowed down, but I just couldn't get my heartrate down. This friend is also a runner and he had trained at the same location enough to know what my pace should be and I was on a sub-twelve minute pace. For me, that was a little too fast. He started screaming at me that I was going to blow up if I didn't slow down and in my mind I knew that, but I was feeling pretty good, even for running below what my pace should have been. I did slow down, but in the next half mile, I started feeling the effects. My heartrate jumped up to about 177 and I slowed down to a crawl. Some of the power walkers were passing me, but that was okay because I wasn't going to stop even if my jog was slower than a walk. I was determined not to break stride. I was happy that I was racing my own race now, unlike the start when I got caught in the pace of everyone else.

At the halfway mark, I was not hurting. I just knew that the fast start had hurt me more than I should have let it. I was a little bit more fatigued than I had anticipated being. But I was still hanging in there, and if I could still shoot for a 45-minute 5K, then that would be okay. Well, after another half mile, I started feeling better. I still had some fatigue, but I was not going to give up. I started focusing on just making each step and to keep moving, still determined not to drop out of my jogging stride and keep fighting for the finish line.

Then I was only a block from the finish line and realized that I wouldn't have as much energy for a kick as I wanted, so I would put off my kick until the last possible moment. I kicked at about 75 yards from the finish line and bumped off a couple of people, which is nothing to brag about, but my kick had gotten me a 45:03. This was just another benchmark in my year of training and despite the lack of training, I was able to get fairly close to my goal.

Success seems to be connected with action. Successful men keep moving. They make mistakes, but they don't quit.
- Conrad Hilton -

The spirit, the will to win, and the will to excel are the things that endure. These qualities are so much more important than the events that occur.
- Vince Lombardi -

- Chapter Fifteen -
Getting Ready For Your First
Triathlon

opefully if you have gotten this book, it's not because my mother forced you to get it and it has shown you that triathlon is not just a sport for the elite. It can be a sport for anyone. You may have to train a long time for your first triathlon or you may have to train a short period, but hopefully you are getting to the point that you are starting to at least see that it is a realistic goal. Even if you are six months or more away, this chapter can give you some input on what to have and what to do at your first triathlon.

If your first triathlon is a short sprint and is billed as a "get your feet wet" event for beginners, don't expect that you will get all of the amenities that you will at a larger event. You might even find that you will just show up the morning of the race and check in and get nothing, but whatever the case, be familiar with the event schedule and when things will occur.

Take into consideration how far away the event is from your home. If the event is more than an hour away, chances are that you will want to spend the night before near the event. I personally don't like to get up early and drive to the event, I like staying in a hotel and being able to relax not having to worry about a long early morning drive. If you have friends competing in the event then you may want to team up and drive, or better yet have your friend drive.

If you are going out of town, don't wait to pack thirty minutes before you leave. Start thinking a week in advance about the items that you need to pack and make a list. I make a list that is categorized by each event and lists what will be needed in each one. Then I make a list of the items that I need for my overnight stay. It never ceases to amaze me the competitors that show up to an event so unprepared. Don't let yourself be put in a position of being unprepared.

What will you need for the swim? Swimsuit or Trisuit, Wetsuit, and goggles. You need to think about what you will wear in the swim. Many people wear Speedos and that's fine, but if you are an overweight athlete, you may not feel comfortable in these. It doesn't matter. I have worn shorts that probably slowed me down, but I was comfortable in them. In most of the triathlons that I have competed, folks don't wear wetsuits, but if you have one, you're comfortable in it and it is legal for this event, knock yourself out. Just remember that if you wear a wetsuit you are going to heat up a lot quicker than if you don't wear one. Sometimes I wear a pair of tri shorts under my swim trunks.

Goggles - bring more than one pair with you. I repeat: bring more than one pair with you. Goggles tend to give you problems when you least expect it even if you have carefully made an inspection and they seem fine.

What will you need for the bike ride? Well, I guess the obvious thing is the bike and your wheels, but at every race someone forgets their bike or a wheel. If you're going to do the bike portion, the complete bike is imperative. You also need other things such as your helmet, gloves, water bottles, socks, bike shoes, spare tube, pump or inflation device. You may want to add your energy bars or gel if you use any of these. If you swam in just shorts you probably will want a shirt to race in.

Now for the last event - the run. I suggest that you wear the same thing on the run as you did on the bike, because it doesn't complicate things. The only thing you will need to have in addition is your running shoes and maybe a hat or cap. Some people like to carry a water bottle or gel and you certainly can add this if you need to.

For your transition area, you will want to consider having the following: a small towel for drying off, a water bottle so you can wash your feet off after you exit the swim, a large towel or a mat for the ground at the transition area. I would also recommend that you have some duct tape, or electrical tape for emergencies.

If you can register and complete packet pickup the day before the race, do it. Larger races won't let you pick up a packet the day of the race. The night before the race, you should lay out all of your gear and make sure that you have everything that is on your list. After you are sure that you have everything , you need to pack it all into a small duffle bag and only leave out what you need to put on the next morning. Go over your bike and make sure that you have good tires and pump up the pressure in the tires to what you will need them to be the next morning. This will allow you to just top the tires off the next morning. Then GET INTO BED EARLY.

The next morning, plan to get up so that you will not be in a rush to get to the race. Plan with enough time so that you can stay relaxed and if anything unexpected happens, you still have time to make alternate plans. Make your way to the transition area to find the spot for your bike and then begin laying out your transition area. After you get the transition area squared away, you will need to go and get your race markings. Usually there is an area that is set up and volunteers will mark race numbers on your body with a permanent marker (Don't worry. It comes off with alcohol or nail polish remover).

By this time, you are getting near to the start of the swim. You should know which wave you will be starting in and be aware of what the time is. Usually you will hear the public address announcer giving you a count down until the start. Once your wave is up, just get ready. Everything you have trained for is going to become apparent. You will be in a group of swimmers who are all excited and ready to get underway. If you are not a confident swimmer, you need to get in the back and move to the side furthest from the first buoy, this will give you less traffic to swim though. Nonetheless, be prepared to get hit, pushed, pulled and kicked at the start, unless you hold way back. Don't get caught up in everyone else's pace. Get into your pace and race your race. Remember you have two more events to go after this one and if this is your first race, face it: you are not going to be in first place. If you are swimming in a lake or ocean, there may be debris, trash, moss or seaweed, so don't let it bother you if you run into an area of it. If there were any little critters in it, they are gone after the first wave. As you come to the finish of the swim, I suggest standing up and walking as quickly as you can. This may sound stupid, but hurry without getting into *too* big of a hurry. If you will slow down just a little, you will make better time than if you are out of control.

At the transition, remain calm and make your transition as smooth and effective as possible. Then walk your bike to the transition area and make sure you are across the mount line before you get on your bike. Also make sure you have your bike helmet fastened, because in most races you could be disqualified or assessed a penalty. As with the swim, race your race and remember that you need to hydrate really well. You have lost fluids on the swim and now is the time that you need to replenish yourself, but don't do it too quickly. Race as smart as you know how and don't spend all of your energy on the bike. You still have one more event when you finish. As you near the end of the bike segment, try spinning in a higher gear so that you can loosen up your legs and prepare for the run. Remember that you will have to dismount usually in the same area where you mounted your bike and walk it back to your transition area.

Change into your running shoes and go, go, go! If you need to walk to get your legs where they feel comfortable, then do whatever it takes. Just keep moving. Usually this is where my mind starts playing games with me and tells me that I can quit, that I don't have anything to prove, that I have made a good effort. This is when you say, "That's a bunch of crap and I've gone this far so I can go the rest of the way!"

Keep plugging along. The finish line is getting closer with every step. When you see it, you won't remember that you are hurting, that anything has gone wrong, or just how slow or fast you are. You will just know that you are going to finish and that was what you set out to do. Don't try to hold back your smile. You should be happy. You completed your first triathlon!

Never give up. Never, never give up!
We shall go on to the end.
- Winston Churchill -

Setting up my transition area

Waiting for the swim start at the
Zyedco Tri.

Crossing the finish line in my 7th triathlon.

Racing to the Finish!

Race Day Check List

- ❑ towels
- ❑ swim cap
- ❑ goggles
- ❑ swimsuit
- ❑ sunscreen
- ❑ racing shorts
- ❑ racing top
- ❑ water bottles
- ❑ bike
- ❑ helmet

- ❑ socks
- ❑ cycling shoes
- ❑ cycling gloves
- ❑ race belt
- ❑ visor or cap
- ❑ running shoes
- ❑ drink mix or sports drink
- ❑ spare tubes
- ❑ directions
- ❑ USAT card

About the Author

Michael Pate is not a professional athlete. He is not a world-famous author with a string of best-selling novels to his credit. He is, however, an exceptional man with a big heart and a never-say-die attitude about every endeavor he undertakes. He is a man who inspires all of those who know him with his optimism and love of life.

This inspiring account of the beginning of his journey towards personal fitness is offered as an encouragement to those who want to make a change but aren't sure how to go about it.

Michael Pate lives in Central Louisiana with his wife Felicia and son Christopher. He is their hero.

To order additional copies or to book the author for a speaking engagement go to www.whenbigboystri.com